Applying
the
BIBLE

Applying the BIBLE

Jack Kuhatschek

ZondervanPublishingHouse

Grand Rapids, Michigan

A Division of HarperCollinsPublishers

Applying the Bible
Copyright © 1990 by Jack Kuhatschek

The book was previously published under the title *Taking the Guesswork Out of Applying the Bible.*

Requests for information should be addressed to:

⛪ ZondervanPublishingHouse
Grand Rapids, Michigan 49530

Library of Congress Cataloging-in-Publication Data

Kuhatschek, Jack, 1949–
   [Taking the guesswork out of applying the Bible]
   Applying the Bible / Jack Kuhatschek.
      p.   cm.
   Originally published: Taking the guesswork out of applying the Bible. Downers
Grove, Ill. : InterVarsity Press, c1990.
   Includes bibliographical references (p.   )
   ISBN: 0-310-20838-6 (softcover)
   1. Bible–use. I. Title.
BS538.3.K84   1996
220.6'01—dc20   95-42151
                                                    CIP

Printed in the United States of America

---

96 97 98 99 00 01 02 03 /❖ DH/ 10 9 8 7 6 5 4 3 2

For
Sandy, Katie and Chris

CONTENTS

THE OTHER HALF OF BIBLE STUDY

N*ot long ago I received a prayer letter concerning a "Miracle Healing Revival."* A Miracle Prayer Request Sheet was enclosed with the following instructions:

Take the prayer sheet I have sent you and write your name on it, and as you do, *lay hands* on it. We must have your prayer requests back from you so we can *touch* them and pray over them for "if any two agree *touching* anything, it shall be done."

Because of their misunderstanding of the King James Version, these well-meaning Christians hit a new low in biblical interpretation and application. The word *touching,* which is so crucial to their viewpoint, does not even occur in the Greek text, as the NIV makes clear in its rendering of the verse: "If two of you on earth agree about anything you ask for, it will be done for you by my Father in heaven" (Mt. 18:19).

Although a bit extreme, this example illustrates the unusual and sometimes-amusing ways the Bible is applied. In this case the faulty application resulted from a misunderstanding of the text. As a professor of mine used to say, many applicational elephants dangle from interpretive threads!

But even when we understand the meaning of a passage, we may not apply it properly. For example, the fourth commandment seems clear enough: "Six days you shall labor and do all your work, but the seventh day is a Sabbath to the LORD your God. On it you shall not do any work" (Ex 20:9-10). Yet today Christians are divided over how to apply this command. Some claim that we should refrain from any work on the Sabbath. Ironically, such people are usually hard at work on Saturday, the day actually set aside in the Old Testament for rest, mowing their yards or working in their gardens! Others claim the command was part of the Old Covenant and is no longer binding. Who is right?

If we turn to the standard books on Bible study, we are given little help with the often-thorny problems of application. One noted author, for example, wrote over two hundred pages on how to study the Bible, but devoted only a page and a half to principles of application. Seemingly embarrassed by this fact, he wrote: "People ask, 'Why is this section on application so short, especially if application is the most important part of Bible study?' "[1] His answer was that if we properly observed and interpreted a passage, then application would be easy.

His response is revealing. Many books on hermeneutics (principles of interpretation) devote hundreds of pages to interpreting the Bible but spend only five or ten on how to apply it.

Typically such books will go to great lengths explaining how to interpret according to the grammatical, cultural, historical and literary aspects of a passage. We learn about figures of speech, typology, symbols, prophecy and poetry. But when it comes to the most important aspect of Bible study, the ultimate goal of all this thoughtful labor, they suddenly run out of things to say!

In recent years the situation has begun to change somewhat. Biblical scholars and theologians have started to wrestle with the sometimes-perplexing problems of applying the Bible to our modern world. Yet even though numerous articles and essays have been written, few of these have been aimed at a popular audience.[2]

When we turn to commentaries, the prospects are not much better. Biblical scholars often do an excellent job of helping us to understand the biblical world. Their commentaries provide a clear explanation of the problems faced by those in Ephesus or Galatia and the answers given by Paul and the other writers of Scripture. But most commentaries make no attempt to relate that message to the modern world. This is regrettable since the job is only half done.

Perhaps it is assumed that application is best done by pastors rather than scholars since it is more "devotional" in nature. Yet John Stott laments that many preachers are far more at home in the biblical than in the modern world. They prefer Jerusalem to their hometowns. He writes:

> We preach biblically. Why, of course, how else could we preach? Charles Simeon and Charles Spurgeon are our heroes. We are determined like them to expound the Scriptures, and to derive all our teaching from God's Word. But . . . our preaching . . . fails to build a bridge into the modern world.

It is biblical but not contemporary. And if we are called to
account for our practice of exposition without application, we
piously reply that our trust is in the Holy Spirit to apply his
Word to the realities of human life.[3]

Of course it would be foolish to think that people fail to apply
the Bible. Every Christian seeks to obey God's Word in daily life.
We do our best to follow the teachings of Scripture in our
families, at work and in our churches. Common sense helps us
to know which teachings are for every age and which were never
intended for us. For example, none of us ever feels obligated to
go to Nicopolis to spend the winter, even though Paul urges
Titus to do that (Tit 3:12). Likewise, we seldom greet our brothers with a holy kiss (1 Thess 5:26), feeling confident that a holy
handshake is sufficient. Yet when Paul tells the Colossians to
"devote yourselves to prayer," we instinctively know that we
should do this too.

Unfortunately, common sense is not always so common (people disagree on how to apply specific passages), and it does not
always make sense (some applications seem foolish). Something
more is needed. We need to take the same care in applying the
Bible as we do in interpreting the Bible. We need to be guided
by sound principles of application, just as we are guided by
sound principles of interpretation.

The purpose of this book is to help us understand *how* to apply
the Bible. In the first half of the book, I discuss principles of
application. I focus especially on those principles which will help
us apply passages which seem outdated or irrelevant to our needs
today. My assumption is that if we can learn a method for applying the more difficult passages, that same method will work
with the easier passages as well.

In the second half of the book, I discuss specific types of application, such as how to apply biblical commands, examples and promises. Some may wonder why I have chosen these three areas rather than dealing with literary genres, such as poetry, prophecy, narrative literature and so on. I chose not to deal with specific genres because there is already an excellent book which does so entitled *How to Read the Bible for All It's Worth.*[4] It also occurred to me that most people do not think in terms of genre and might feel more comfortable with the categories of commands, examples and promises. Although these three categories are not intended to be exhaustive, they are representative of the kinds of applications we most often make in Scripture. In discussing them I have tried to draw examples from most of the major genres in Scripture.

Of course, it is impossible to talk about application without also discussing interpretation. For that reason, I have devoted an earlier chapter to interpreting the Bible. In addition, most chapters will touch on certain aspects of interpretation before discussing a particular facet of application. I make no apologies for the brevity of this discussion in proportion to the rest of the book. There are dozens of books on Bible study which cover the subject thoroughly. I have devoted the majority of the book to the theory and practice of application, just as typical books on Bible study devote the majority of their material to interpretation.

However, before proceeding further I need to describe the nature and limits of this book. First, the title: *Taking the Guesswork out of Applying the Bible.* I blush a little when I read it. It would be ludicrous to assume that application can somehow become a precise science with all guesswork removed. Application is an art and a spiritual discipline which cannot be fully reduced to a set of rules or principles. Yet I do believe some of the guesswork can be eliminated by the principles and methods described in this book.

Second, by focusing on some of the rules and principles which may be helpful in application, a book could become overly analytical or intellectual about God's Word. The Bible does not have to be analyzed or reduced to general principles in order to have an impact on our lives. People were being transformed by Scripture long before there were commentaries, atlases or books on hermeneutics. The narrative and poetic portions of Scripture reach far deeper than our intellect, and their impact cannot be analyzed or quantified. For that very reason, however, I have tried to focus on those aspects of application which *can* be discussed and evaluated, freely admitting that this is only part of the story. Since this book is not intended for scholars, I have tried to present a complex subject as clearly as possible. In so doing, I may have erred on the side of simplicity.

Finally, I must confess that this book is only a first step in trying to understand and explain the nature of application to the general reader. Although I consulted many helpful sources as I wrote, I was only able to find one book devoted exclusively to application, and its approach was quite different from mine.[5] Recently, I have become aware of two other manuscripts on application, but to my knowledge neither has yet been published. At times, therefore, I felt I was stepping out without a guide into unknown territory. I believe I have made some progress, but I truly hope that other and better books will be written on this subject in the future. My desire is that we will all gain a clearer idea of how to live out the teachings of Scripture.

PART 1

PRINCIPLES
OF
APPLICATION

THE GOAL
OF
APPLICATION

W*hile studying in the Holy Lands, a seminary professor of mine* met a man who claimed to have memorized the Old Testament—in Hebrew! Needless to say, the astonished professor asked for a demonstration. A few days later they sat together in the man's home.

"Where shall we begin?" asked the man.

"Psalm 1," replied my professor, who was an avid student of the psalms.

Beginning with Psalm 1:1, the man began to recite from memory, while my professor followed along in his Hebrew Bible. For two hours the man continued word for word without a mistake as the professor sat in stunned silence.

When the demonstration was over, my professor discovered something even more astonishing about the man—he was an *atheist!* Here was someone who knew the Scriptures better than most Christians ever will, and yet he didn't even believe in God.

At the other end of the spectrum, I have known people who have immersed themselves in Scripture and have become living illustrations of God's Word. As Paul says, they are "letter[s] from Christ" for everyone to read, letters "written not with ink but with the Spirit of the living God" (2 Cor 3:3).

One couple in particular stands out in my mind. Jim and Martha have an intimate relationship with Christ, and when they greet you, their faces radiate love and acceptance. In fact, acceptance is too weak a word. They make you feel special, whether you're "somebody" or not. Martha's standard greeting is, "I'm so glad to *see* you!" She says it with such sincerity and enthusiasm that you are tempted to look behind you to see whether the pastor or the president of the college just came through the door! When you realize she really is speaking to you, you begin to feel honored—and that's exactly what you are.

Although Jim and Martha minister publicly on a regular basis, I'm most impressed by their "quiet ministry" done behind the scenes. They often invite home people whom others neglect: international students, singles, those who have emotional or spiritual problems and those who are socially awkward. (My wife and I have been in their home many times!)

The atheist and these two committed Christians have very different responses to Scripture. To use one person's analogy, the atheist is like a bad photograph—overexposed and underdeveloped! He knows Scripture but refuses to let it affect his life. Jim and Martha, though enthusiastic students of the Bible, by

no means know it by heart. Even so, what they know they take
to heart.

Most Christians, however, are somewhere between the atheist
and Jim and Martha. They are exposed to Scripture regularly in
church, Sunday school, home Bible studies and their daily de-
votions. They know many of the teachings of Scripture, but their
lives fail to demonstrate the spiritual maturity we all desire.

Knowledge of the Bible is obviously not enough. Something
more is needed for the truths of Scripture to transform our lives.
In this chapter we will seek to discover what that "something
more" is.

A Spiritual Diagnosis

In 1 Corinthians 2:14—3:4 Paul introduces us to four types of
people: those "without the Spirit" (2:14), those who are "infants
in Christ" (3:1), those who are "spiritual" (2:15) and those who
are "worldly" (3:1). Each of us falls into one of these categories.

Those without the Spirit. The atheist mentioned earlier obviously fits into this category. He was a remarkable man, but Scripture
had no impact on his life. Paul tells us why: "The man without
the Spirit does not accept the things that come from the Spirit
of God, for they are foolishness to him, and he cannot understand them, because they are spiritually discerned" (1 Cor 2:14).

We must be careful how we interpret Paul's words, especially
the statement "he cannot understand them." Does this mean that
a non-Christian is incapable of reading and grasping the meaning of biblical passages? I think not. James Sire, author of *The
Universe Next Door,* claims that he met an amazing student at one
of his evangelistic lectures. As other non-Christians would object to some of the beliefs of Christianity, this student would

interrupt and say, "No, you've got it all wrong. Christians don't believe that." Then he would go on to explain clearly and accurately what Christians do believe. "His theology was impeccably orthodox," says Sire. "He just didn't believe any of it!"

Paul is not speaking of mental comprehension only, the kind that an English professor might have of a Shakespearean play. Rather, he intends something deeper, more profound—an understanding that both illuminates our minds and transforms our spirits. This kind of understanding requires the Spirit of God.

Those who are infants in Christ. Unlike the atheist or the non-Christian student, new Christians have the Holy Spirit living in them. What a difference he makes! Suddenly the Bible is no longer foolish and unacceptable. It seems fresh, exciting, full of relevance and challenge. But the Bible hasn't changed; we have.

I still remember the night I became a Christian. I was seventeen and attended a Billy Graham film called *The Restless Ones.* After going forward at the end of the film, I was instructed to go home and read the Gospel of John. Later that night, after everyone else was in bed, I looked all over the house for a Bible (we weren't a religious family). I finally found a Gideon Bible my father had taken from a motel. It took me a few minutes to find John's Gospel, but when I found it I began to read eagerly. A few days later I purchased a Phillips Version of the New Testament, read it from cover to cover and continued to read it every day. At night I would lie in bed with a pocket radio, listening to religious broadcasts. I simply couldn't get enough of Scripture!

In spite of my eagerness and enthusiasm, however, I was not yet what Paul would call a spiritual Christian. Like a newborn baby, I had a tremendous appetite for Scripture, but my capacity to understand and apply God's Word was limited.

Those who are spiritual. Some Christians claim that a spiritual Christian is simply one who is filled with the Spirit. According to this view, even infants in Christ instantly can become spiritual by asking the Spirit to fill them. This view fails to notice, however, that in both 1 Corinthians 2—3 and Hebrews 5:11-14 those who are spiritual are able to eat the "solid food" of Scripture because they have matured beyond infancy. Babies can't eat solid food no matter how healthy they are. Rather, those who are infants in Christ must drink the "milk" of the Word.

Spiritual Christians, therefore, are characterized by two things: spiritual maturity and a greater capacity to understand God's Word. These two qualities are closely related. It isn't simply that mature Christians happen to know a lot of Scripture. Rather, they have allowed the Spirit of God to use the Word of God to bring them from infancy to maturity.

Jim and Martha, the couple mentioned earlier, fit into this category. They don't merely know Scripture, they *live* Scripture. Over the years they have allowed the Spirit of God to mold and shape them to the point where they are vivid examples of biblical truths.

Those who are worldly. The other day I was at the park with my daughter, Katie. As I was pushing her in a swing, another father came over with his son. Although the boy was much older than Katie, he was mentally handicapped. As a result, he functioned like someone half his age.

We view someone who is mentally retarded as "abnormal." Yet somehow we accept spiritual retardation as normal. Our churches are full of Christians who have known the Lord for many years. Yet many of these Christians have never grown spiritually as they have aged chronologically. They are spiritual infants in adult bodies. How tragic! The author of Hebrews describes them well:

> We have much to say about this, but it is hard to explain because you are slow to learn. In fact, though by this time you ought to be teachers, you need someone to teach you the elementary truths of God's word all over again. You need milk, not solid food! Anyone who lives on milk, being still an infant, is not acquainted with the teaching about righteousness. But solid food is for the mature, who by constant use have trained themselves to distinguish good from evil. (Heb 5:11-14)

How can we avoid the tragedy of spiritual retardation? What must we do to grow into spiritual maturity? The author of Hebrews suggests that we go into training!

A Spiritual Training Program

Those of us who have grown up in the Western Hemisphere have a strange and unbiblical view of knowledge. We have been taught that knowledge can be divorced from commitment and action. We are told that we must remain detached, aloof, objective if we truly want to know something.

Those in the ancient Near East, the world of the Bible, would consider such detachment nonsense. They would claim that true knowledge is impossible apart from commitment, involvement and action. We must immerse ourselves in our subject if we want to know it. Proverbs 2:3-5 suggests: "If you call out for insight and cry aloud for understanding, and if you look for it as for silver and search for it as for hidden treasure, then you will understand the fear of the LORD and find the knowledge of God."

My experience has confirmed the truth of the Eastern model. For example, a few years ago I decided to learn how to fish. I borrowed a fishing rod and some lures from a friend and went to a nearby lake. Over and over I cast the lure into the water, expecting a fish to grab it at any moment. Two hours later, I hadn't even gotten a nibble.

That evening I went to the store to buy a magazine on fishing. I read it from cover to cover, absorbing every fact I could find about how to catch fish. I discovered that you must match a lure to the type of fish and the type of fishing conditions. Armed with my new knowledge, I went back the next evening to try again. Although I still didn't have much luck, I managed to catch what some would call an overgrown minnow. Despite its size, I was elated!

Over the next few weeks I kept reading and fishing, fishing and reading, trying out every new bit of information I found. Again and again I found that my knowledge had to be tempered with experience if I was to be successful. After a while I was bringing home large stringers of fish while others were leaving empty-handed.

The same is true in every area of life. Olympic athletes train for years to perfect their skills. Doctors undergo demanding internships and residencies. Pilots spend hours in flight simulators before actually flying an aircraft. In each case their knowledge must be joined with experience in order to achieve the desired result.

If this is true of every other area of life, why should we expect it to be different in the spiritual sphere? In the words of the author of Hebrews, we must train ourselves through constant practice to distinguish good from evil. Or, as James puts it:

Do not merely listen to the word, and so deceive yourselves. Do what it says. Anyone who listens to the word but does not do what it says is like a man who looks at his face in a mirror and, after looking at himself, goes away and immediately forgets what he looks like. But the man who looks intently into the perfect law that gives freedom, and continues to do this, not forgetting what he has heard, but doing it—he will be blessed in what he does. (1:22-25)

In both the Old and New Testaments, the Bible is emphatic about the relationship between knowledge and action. If we want to mature spiritually, therefore, we must act on what we know.

Use It or Lose It!

When I was ten years old, my father and I took up amateur ("ham") radio as a hobby. We both learned the basics of Morse code and took a simple test to get our novice licenses. Pretty soon we were talking in code to other radio operators around the world. The walls of the room from which we transmitted were covered with postcards from England, South America and even Madagascar.

By the time I was eleven, we began studying for our general-class licenses. This was no piece of cake. The textbook we had to master was about two inches thick. We had to learn the basics of electronics and numerous FCC rules of communication, and we had to increase our knowledge of Morse code from five to thirteen words per minute. During the code part of the exam, we had to send and receive code at that speed for five minutes without error. The written part of the exam took over an hour. My father passed the test fairly easily. It took me three attempts, but I finally became the youngest general-class operator in Texas!

That was twenty-eight years ago. Today when I hear Morse code, I don't hear a message—I hear noise! Because I stopped using it, I lost most of what I knew.

In Matthew 13:12-15 Jesus states this as a spiritual principle: Whoever does not have, even what he has will be taken from him. This is why I speak to them in parables: Though seeing, they do not see; though hearing, they do not hear or understand. In them is fulfilled the prophecy of Isaiah: "You will be ever hearing but never understanding; you will be ever seeing but never perceiving. For this people's heart has become calloused; they hardly hear with their ears, and they have closed their eyes. Otherwise they might see with their eyes, hear with their ears, understand with their hearts and turn, and I would heal them."

As Bible study editor for InterVarsity Press, I find this principle a bit scary. Virtually every day I spend hours reading Scripture as I edit the Bible-study guides we publish. At times my senses become dulled as I try to process that much information. My greatest fear is that reading God's Word will turn into a mechanical process, a mindless and heartless routine to get the job done. Jesus warns that those who fail to respond to Scripture can lose their spiritual senses. We can become spiritually blind and deaf if we fail to practice what we learn. God's Word will continue to sound its alarm, but we will go on sleeping, like someone who has hit the snooze button too many times.

Fortunately, the converse is also true: "Whoever has will be given more, and he will have an abundance" (Mt 13:12). As we use our spiritual eyes, our eyesight will improve. As we use our spiritual ears, our hearing will become more acute. As we respond to the light God has given us, he will give us more and more light until our lives are flooded with the glory of God.

The Goal of Application

As we immerse ourselves in Scripture, our goal is to develop within ourselves the mind and heart of God. We want to be able to think and to respond to every situation the way God himself would.

Is this an impossible goal? The Lord does warn us in Isaiah:

". . . My thoughts are not your thoughts, neither are your ways my ways," declares the LORD. "As the heavens are higher than the earth, so are my ways higher than your ways and my thoughts than your thoughts." (Is 55:8-9)

Yet this state of affairs was neither God's original intention nor his ultimate plan. Genesis tells us that originally "God created man in his own image, in the image of God he created him" (1:27). Although this divine image was defaced and distorted by the Fall, it is in the process of being restored by Christ.

This theme is reiterated throughout the Bible, especially in the New Testament. Paul tells us that we have "taken off [our] old self with its practices and have put on the new self, which is being renewed in knowledge in the *image* of its Creator" (Col 3:9-10, italics mine). In Ephesians 4:24 he writes that our new selves are "created to be *like God* in true righteousness and holiness." In Romans 8:29 we read, ". . . Those God foreknew he also predestined to be conformed to the *likeness* of his Son, that he might be the firstborn among many brothers." Just as Jesus

Christ is the "image of the invisible God" (Col 1:15), so too we will one day, in a secondary sense, be recreated in God's image.

How do we achieve this seemingly unreachable goal? We do so first through the broad study of Scripture. Although God's thoughts are not our thoughts and his ways are not our ways, he has revealed his thoughts and ways to us in the Bible. As we read Scripture, therefore, we need to look for the mind and character of God to be shown in and behind the details of Scripture. As Fee and Stuart have put it, "In the final analysis, God is the hero of all biblical narratives."[1]

It is exciting to realize, however, that this knowledge of Scripture is not intended merely to fill our minds, like an endless list of do's and don'ts. Rather these external words on the pages of Scripture are to be internalized, written on our hearts by the Holy Spirit. Centuries before Christ, the Lord promised through Jeremiah:

> "The time is coming," declares the LORD, "when I will make a new covenant with the house of Israel and with the house of Judah. . . . This is the covenant I will make with the house of Israel after that time," declares the LORD. *"I will put my law in their minds and write it on their hearts.* I will be their God, and they will be my people. No longer will a man teach his neighbor, or a man his brother, saying, 'Know the LORD,' because they will all know me, from the least of them to the greatest. (31:31-34, italics mine)

Having God's Law written on our hearts means far more than merely committing Scripture to memory. It is the biblical way of saying that our innermost being takes on the character of Scripture, which is the character of God himself. From God's heart to Scripture to our hearts is the divinely intended sequence.

Is this merely the promise of some future age when Christ returns? Is it merely a hope which cannot be realized in our fallen world? No, Paul makes it clear that the process has already begun in the life of every Christian. In 2 Corinthians he echoes the words of Jeremiah when he says, "You show that you are a letter from Christ, the result of our ministry, written not with ink but with the Spirit of the living God, not on tablets of stone but on tablets of human hearts" (3:3). In Romans he declares that we are undergoing a transformation (12:1-2), a metamorphosis (the essence of the Greek word). This metamorphosis is a miraculous, spiritual process. As we renew our minds with Scripture, being careful to put its teachings into practice, we are transformed from spiritual caterpillars to beautiful butterflies who reflect the grace and glory of Jesus Christ. This is the goal of application!

CHAPTER TWO

LEARNING
TO APPLY
GOD'S WORD

*M*any people consider the Bible hopelessly outdated and irrelevant. This was brought home to me several years ago when I listened to a comedian imitate a preacher. In a high-pitched, snooty voice, he passionately expounded his text, arriving ultimately at the climax of his sermon—the application:

Life, dear friends, is like a tin of sardines. We peel back the top and partake of the sardines, the riches of life. But you know, there's always a little piece in the corner we can't get at! Is there a piece in the corner of *your* life? I know there is in mine. At such times I urge you to turn for comfort to the words of our text: "My brother Esau is an hairy man, but I am a smooth man."[1]

Of course his application was absurd, and it had absolutely no connection to the "text." But that's the point! People wonder what benefit we can possibly derive from a two-thousand-year-old book written in an obscure corner of the Middle East.

In a sense I can't blame them. After all, much of the Bible does seem irrelevant today. For example, in Galatians Paul devotes several chapters to circumcision, demonstrating that it isn't necessary for salvation. That's a gripping subject! When was the last time anyone urged you to be circumcised as a means of salvation?

Or consider 1 Corinthians 8, Paul's thrilling passage about food sacrificed to idols. After reading that chapter, we are convinced that we should never eat idol meat around a "weaker brother." Then it dawns on us that no one sells idol meat today. Of course if they did, we would avoid it like the plague! But the problem simply doesn't exist in our culture.

There are perhaps hundreds of examples of seemingly outdated biblical material. Consider the pages and pages devoted to the genealogies in Genesis, the construction of the tabernacle in Exodus, the details about animal sacrifices in Leviticus and the almost endless lists of names in Numbers and Chronicles. Is it any wonder that those who try to read straight through the Bible often get bogged down, especially in the "pots and pans" sections of Leviticus?

Please don't misunderstand me. I'm not saying these portions of Scripture are irrelevant. They simply *seem* irrelevant. I am committed to Paul's view of the Bible: "All Scripture is God-breathed and is useful for teaching, rebuking, correcting and training in righteousness, so that the man of God may be thoroughly equipped for every good work" (2 Tim 3:16-17). All of the Bible is useful, not useless—even those passages mentioned above.

Yet if God's Word is eternally relevant, then why did he include so many passages that seem outdated today? To answer this question we need to consider the nature of Scripture.

God's Word: Timely, Yet Timeless

God's Word is timely. He spoke to *specific* situations, problems and questions. He promised Abraham a son (Gen 15). He revealed to Joseph the meaning of Pharaoh's dream (Gen 41). He called Moses to lead his people out of Egypt (Ex 3). Through Nathan, he exposed David's sin with Bathsheba (2 Sam 12). He warned Nineveh that they would be destroyed unless they repented (Jon 3). Throughout the Bible God becomes personally involved in people's lives. He doesn't offer pious platitudes but rather speaks directly to their needs in ways that are appropriate to their situations.

This is good because we are given examples which are *concrete* rather than abstract. God could have given us a theological treatise on the problem of pain and suffering. Instead he gave us the book of Job. We feel Job's pain and identify with his struggles. God could have inspired a lengthy discourse on the nature of faith. Instead he called Abram out of Ur and allows us to watch the drama of this man's life and his growing ability to trust God. The beauty and intensity of the Psalms is a direct result of their concrete nature. They record the joy, sorrow, anger and praise of people caught up in the passion of everyday life.

But the concrete nature of Scripture also creates problems. Our situations, problems and questions are not always directly related to theirs. Therefore, God's word to them does not always seem immediately relevant to us. For example, God hasn't called us to leave Ur of the Chaldeans. We aren't being held captive in Egypt. The destruction of Jericho and Ai make for exciting reading, but we hardly feel compelled to circle Chicago or Los Angeles seven times!

Fortunately, Scripture is not only timely but timeless. Just as God spoke to the original audience, so he still speaks to us through the pages of Scripture. Because we share a common humanity with the people of the Bible, we discover a *universal* dimension in the problems they faced and the solutions God gave them. We may not know anyone named Bathsheba, but we struggle with lust, and adultery is all too common. We may not rule over Nineveh, but, like Belshazzar, we sometimes feel proud and arrogant, not realizing that God holds in his hand our life and all our ways (Dan 5:23). We may not have the same "thorn" that tormented Paul, but as we pray for hardships to be removed from our lives we need to hear God's words: "My grace is sufficient for you, for my power is made perfect in weakness" (2 Cor 12:9).

The timeless nature of Scripture is obvious in many passages. When the Bible tells us to "honor your father and mother" (Eph 6:2), we know this applies today. Likewise, when Paul describes "the most excellent way" of love in 1 Corinthians 13, we feel sure he is speaking to us, not just to the Corinthians.

These passages and hundreds of others apply to us directly. Because our situations are virtually identical to those faced by the original readers, God's Word to us is the same as it was to them. Fathers and mothers are a part of every time and culture, and children are to respect and obey them. And no matter where or when we live, love is the foundation of human relationships.

But how do we apply those passages that seem outdated and irrelevant, those which were so timely that they appear to have lost their timeless dimension? How can we apply portions of Scripture that were written to questions, needs and problems we no longer face?

Learning from the Ox

Imagine that you are having your quiet time in Deuteronomy. As you come to the chapters describing miscellaneous laws for Israel (great when you can't sleep), you read: "Do not muzzle an ox while it is treading out the grain" (Deut 25:4). Now if you happen to be a farmer who uses oxen, this may be an exciting moment. It never dawned on you how unfairly you have been treating your oxen. After all, they are out there in the heat of the day, working hard so you can earn a living. But would you let them eat while they work? *No.* (Shame on you!) From that moment you vow never again to muzzle your oxen while they work. But if you're not a farmer (or you use a mechanical thresher), you may simply read on, assuming that this doesn't apply to you.

I mention this passage because it is an example of a situation that is very dissimilar from our own. Most of us don't own oxen—or muzzles for that matter! Therefore, God's command about the ox seems totally irrelevant to our needs. Why, then, did God include that verse in Scripture? If we can answer that question, and find a way to truly apply that verse today, we may be able to apply many other perplexing passages.

It turns out that the apostle Paul once had his quiet time in this passage, and he came away excited by what he discovered. The Corinthians had accused the apostles of being freeloaders taking advantage of the hospitality of others without paying for it. This was a serious charge, one that could hinder the work of the gospel in Corinth and other cities as well.

Paul used several analogies to argue that the apostles had the right to receive financial support: "Who serves as a soldier at his own expense? Who plants a vineyard and does not eat of its grapes? Who tends a flock and does not drink of the milk?" (1 Cor 9:7). But he wanted to prove his point from Scripture. This verse was what he needed. "Do I say this merely from a human point of view? Doesn't the Law say the same thing? For it is written in the Law of Moses: 'Do not muzzle an ox while it is treading out the grain' " (vv. 8-9).

At first glance this may seem like proof-texting. Paul needed a verse, so he merely pulled one out of context to support his position. But that is not the case.[2] It is clear that Paul understood the *original situation* described in the verse and why God gave the command about the ox. He writes: ". . . When the plowman plows and the thresher threshes, they ought to do so in the hope of sharing in the harvest" (v. 10).

Those of us who did not grow up in a primitive agrarian society have greater difficulty than Paul in understanding the verse. The *Handbook of Life in Bible Times* helps us to cross this cultural barrier:

> Small quantities of grain (and more delicate crops such as dill or cumin) were beaten with rods cut from a tree. Larger quantities were threshed by allowing animals to trample over them, although oxen were not allowed to be muzzled so that they too could share in the harvest while they worked.[3]

In other words, since the ox was helping to thresh the grain, he deserved to share in the harvest too. But instead of being paid at the end of the harvest, the ox is granted permission to use the eat-as-you-go payment plan!

Notice, however, that Paul's statements about the verse go beyond its original application. The verse only mentions oxen; Paul mentions plowmen and threshers. Where did they come from? Having thought about the verse, Paul realized that the command about the ox was merely one specific application of a *broader principle,* namely that animals and people have a right to be paid for their work.

It was probably at this point that Paul became excited about his discovery. He undoubtedly underlined the verse in red and put a star in the margin next to it. He realized that this general principle could apply to *his situation* and that of the other apostles as well: "If we have sown spiritual seed among you, is it too much if we reap a material harvest from you? If others have this right of support from you, shouldn't we have it all the more?" (vv. 11-12).

Based on this seemingly obscure verse in Deuteronomy, Paul had a legitimate answer to the accusations of those in Corinth. Yet his application was faithful to the original context and demonstrated insight into the principle behind the command.

Paul's handling of this passage provides a model for applying other passages which seem outdated or irrelevant today. First, we must understand the *original situation* described in the passage and how God's Word applied to that situation (the ox's right to eat).

Second, we must determine whether God's Word in that situation reflects a specific application of a *broader principle* (a worker's right to be paid).

Finally, we are ready to apply that general principle to *situations we face* (ministers' right to be paid for their work).

A Thorny Passage

Let's look at another passage which illustrates this approach. In 2 Corinthians 12:1-10 Paul writes about his troublesome "thorn," the "messenger of Satan" used to "torment" him (v. 7). At first glance we wonder whether such an intensely personal and specific problem has any application today. But by following the steps outlined above, we will see that it clearly does.

First, we must seek to understand *Paul's situation* and God's Word to him in that situation. As an apostle, Paul had experienced "surpassingly great revelations" (v. 7), including being "caught up to the third heaven . . . to paradise" (vv. 2, 4). There he "heard inexpressible things, things that man is not permitted to tell" (v. 4). Such experiences were so incredible, so extraordinary that Paul struggled with pride. As an apostle he knew he was a member of Christ's most elite corps. And his spiritual experiences were so spectacular that even the other apostles, not to mention "ordinary Christians," were tempted to envy him. But before he had a chance to become conceited, to soar aloft with feelings of superiority, God nailed his feet to earth: "To keep me from becoming conceited because of these surpassingly great revelations, there was given me a thorn in my flesh, a messenger of Satan, to torment me" (v. 7).

For centuries people have speculated about the precise nature of Paul's thorn. They have suggested it was headaches, earaches, eye disease or malarial fever. Others have claimed it was epilepsy, a speech impediment, hypochondria, deafness or remorse for persecuting Christians. Still others have suggested gallstones, gout, rheumatism, a dental infection—even lice!

Whatever it was, Paul didn't like it. "Three times I pleaded with the Lord to take it away from me" (v. 8). The thorn not only kept Paul humble, it tormented him and made him feel weak. So he prayed and prayed for its removal.

God's answer surprised Paul: "But he said to me, 'My grace is sufficient for you, for my power is made perfect in weakness' " (v. 9). Instead of removing Paul's thorn, God gave him the grace to endure it. Instead of taking away Paul's weakness, God used it to demonstrate his power.

Having understood Paul's situation, our next step is to discover whether God's answer to Paul was a specific application of a *broader principle* that can apply to us. If we look carefully, we notice that this is the case. God's answer goes beyond Paul's immediate situation—and beyond Paul himself. The Lord did not say, "My power is made perfect in your *thorn*" but rather, "My power is made perfect in *weakness*" (v. 9). Paul realized this when he responded, "Therefore I will boast all the more gladly about my weaknesses [plural], so that Christ's power may rest on me" (v. 9). In other words, it doesn't matter whether we can identify the precise nature of Paul's thorn. God's promise applies to anything which makes us feel weak, humble and dependent on God.

Finally, we are ready to apply that general principle to *other situations* which are similar to Paul's thorn. Normally we must do this on our own, but in this passage Paul himself gives us several examples: "That is why, for Christ's sake, I delight in weaknesses, in insults, in hardships, in persecutions, in difficulties. For when I am weak, then I am strong" (v. 10). None of the items in Paul's list is exactly the same as his thorn. But because they shared certain points of similarity with the consequences of his thorn, Paul knew God's grace was sufficient for them all.

The same is true today. We probably don't suffer from the same kind of thorn Paul did. But we too face weaknesses, insults, hardships, persecutions and difficulties—things which humble us and make us dependent on God. Whatever the nature of our thorn, like Paul we can confidently rely on Christ's grace and power.

As Easy as One, Two, Three

Our success in applying Scripture, especially those passages that seem irrelevant today, depends on our skill in following the three steps outlined in this chapter. Yet knowing *what* to do is not the same as knowing *how* to do it. How do we understand the original situation described in a book or passage? How do we discover general principles from the specific commands given to those in the Bible? And how can we know whether a general principle can be legitimately applied to our situation today? These questions will be addressed more fully in the following chapters.

CHAPTER THREE

STEP ONE:
UNDERSTANDING THE
ORIGINAL SITUATION

*I*n a movie called Back to the Future, *a teen-ager from the 1980s*
enters a time machine (a modified DeLorean car) and speeds
down a flaming path back to the 1950s. The town is the same,
but everything has changed. Girls wear ponytails and bobby
socks and say things like, "Isn't he a dream boat!" Guys have oily,
slicked-back hair and wear letter sweaters and baggy pants. As
a car with white sidewall tires pulls into a service station, uni-
formed attendants rush out to fill the tank, clean the windshield
and check the oil. Gas is nineteen cents a gallon, and Cokes are
five cents. As we watch the movie, we are struck with how odd
life used to be and how much things have changed!

We also realize how many things are the same. Being a teen-ager is as awkward now as then. We still have school, homework, parties, friendships and first love. People still cruise down the road with their favorite music blaring from the radio. Little boys will *always* tease their sisters, and although Coke is no longer five cents, people still love to drink it. What's so different?

We have a similar experience when we read the Bible. Many things seem strange or unfamiliar. People wear sandals, ride camels and live in tents. They offer animal sacrifices and consider pork "unclean." They worship on Saturday and work on Sunday. When a woman can't have children, she allows her husband to marry her female servant. What a different world!

Of course, many things seem just the same. The people in the Bible struggle with temptation and have difficulty trusting God. So do we. We identify with Job's suffering, even though he lived four thousand years ago. Husbands still need to love their wives, and children still need to obey their parents. Many times we feel that the biblical writers are speaking directly to us, giving us encouragement, comfort and hope.

The strange-yet-familiar feelings we have when reading the Bible (or watching a movie about the '50s) are a result of *historical distance*. Although we have much in common with the people in the Bible, there is a two- to four-thousand-year gap between us and them. They lived in a different time, a different place, a different culture, and they spoke a different language.

We cannot ignore this historical and cultural distance if we want to understand and apply the Bible.

Becoming a Time Traveler

In a sense, studying and applying the Bible is like entering a time machine. We must cross the barriers of time, language, culture and geography in order to understand the people of the Bible and how God's Word applied to the situations *they* faced. How we do that is the goal of this chapter.

Then, when we have understood how God's Word applied to the people of that century, we re-enter the time machine and return to the twentieth century. Now we are able to reflect on how God's Word applies to our time and culture and the problems *we* face. That will be the goal of later chapters.

Our time machine is constructed from the various tools available to the modern student of the Bible. With these tools we can cross the barriers which separate us from the biblical world.

Crossing the time barrier. Because the events of the Bible took place thousands of years ago, we have one obvious problem in understanding those events—we weren't there! Therefore, we often lack important information regarding the historical context in which those events took place.

For example, almost every New Testament letter was written to address a particular problem or set of problems: the Galatians were seeking to be justified by law; the Corinthians wanted answers to questions about marriage, spiritual gifts, meat offered to idols and so on; Timothy needed to know how to restore order to a church.

Unless we understand these problems or questions, the letters are like listening to one end of a telephone conversation. We hear what the author is saying, but we don't know *why* he is saying it. The same is true when we read the Psalms and Prophets. We know only half of the story!

For example, in John's first epistle he writes:

Dear friends, do not believe every spirit, but test the spirits to see whether they are from God, because many false prophets have gone out into the world. This is how you can recognize the Spirit of God: Every spirit that acknowledges that Jesus Christ has come in the flesh is from God, but every spirit that does not acknowledge Jesus is not from God." (1 Jn 4:1-3)

This passage has often been misinterpreted as a test for demon possession. As a result, it has also been misapplied. We are told that whenever we encounter someone who may be demon possessed, we are to "test the spirits" by asking the person, "Has Jesus Christ come in the flesh?" If the person is possessed by an evil spirit, he or she will respond "No." But if the person answers "Yes," then we can rule out demon possession.

Unfortunately, this is a classic case of interpreting a passage apart from its historical context. A more careful reading of the text reveals that John is not giving a test for demon possession but rather for telling a genuine prophet from a false prophet (v. 1). And the false prophets he has in mind were ones who were denying that the divine Christ had truly become human, since they believed that "flesh" and matter were evil.

How do we know this? There are several ways to learn about the historical context of this or any passage. One way is to look for clues within the book or passage itself. For example, in 1 John 2:19 we discover that these false prophets had originally been part of the church: "They went out from us, but they did not really belong to us" (2:19). John calls them "antichrists" (2:18). One purpose of his letter is to warn his readers about them: "I am writing these things to you about those who are trying to lead you astray" (2:26). There are many other statements in John's letter, some explicit and some implicit, which give us additional details about the situation his readers faced and why he wrote to them.

Once we have looked within the book or passage itself, it is helpful to consult a Bible dictionary or handbook. For example, under the listing "John, Epistles of" in *The New Bible Dictionary* we read that his first epistle

> was called forth by the activities of false teachers who had seceded from the church (or churches) to which John is writing, and who were attempting to seduce the faithful (ii. 18f., 26). They formed an esoteric group, believing that they had superior knowledge to ordinary Christians (cf. ii. 20, 27; 2 Jn. 9) and showing little love to them (cf. iv. 20).
>
> They were forerunners of the later heretics generally known as "Gnostics" (from Gk. *gnosis*, meaning "knowledge") and claimed a special knowledge of God and of theology. On the basis of their new doctrine they appear to have denied that Jesus was the Christ (ii. 22), the pre-existent (i. 1) Son of God (iv. 15, v. 5, 10) come in the flesh (iv. 2; 2 Jn. 7) to provide salvation for men (iv. 9f., 14).[1]

As we seek to discover the historical context of a book or passage, it is also a good idea to read related passages in the Bible. For example, Psalm 51 was written by David after his adultery with Bathsheba. We can read about David and Bathsheba in 2 Samuel 11—12. (The heading over Psalm 51 tells us why it was written. When such information isn't given, a Bible dictionary or commentary will often mention related passages.) Similarly, if we study the book of Philippians, we will want to consult the book of Acts, which provides information about the founding of the church at Philippi (Acts 16).

The more we know about the historical context of a biblical passage, the better equipped we will be to understand the message of the author. Such information can be like finding missing pieces of a puzzle. As they are put into place, the whole picture becomes much clearer.

Crossing the language barrier. The fact that the Bible was written in Hebrew, Aramaic and Greek instead of English creates a significant barrier to understanding its message. Anyone who tries to learn these languages quickly realizes how difficult they are to master. Fortunately, those who are experts in biblical languages have, for the most part, crossed this barrier for us by translating the biblical languages into modern English. In fact, there are numerous Bible translations to choose from.

There are literal translations such as the New American Standard Bible and the Revised Standard Version. There are dynamic-equivalence translations such as the New International Version, the New English Bible and the Good News Bible. And there are free translations such as the Living Bible and the New Testament in Modern English (J. B. Phillips).

Each type of translation has strengths and weaknesses. A literal translation follows the wording of Hebrew or Greek as closely as possible, but such wording often sounds awkward in English.

A free translation is more concerned with clarity than exact wording. Such translations are easy to read but give the impression that the Bible was written in the twentieth century. For example, in the Living Bible's translation of Psalm 119:105, the word *lamp* is translated as "flashlight"!

Dynamic-equivalence translations are probably the best choice. They don't try to update matters of history or culture (a lamp is a lamp, not a flashlight). But they translate the biblical words and phrases into clear and contemporary equivalents in

English. As a result they are easy to read and faithful to the original message.

The smart Bible student will take advantage of all three types of translations. Each one can provide unique insights into what the author originally said in his own language.

It is best, however, to use either literal or dynamic-equivalence translations such as the NIV, RSV and NASB as the basis for our study. These translations allow us to interpret the passage on our own rather than doing much of the work for us. Then, after we have grasped the basic meaning of the passage, a free translation can help to further clarify what the author is saying to his original readers.[2]

Crossing the cultural barrier. The events in the Bible took place in many different cultures: Egyptian, Canaanite, Babylonian, Jewish, Greek and Roman (to name a few). It is not uncommon, therefore, to read about customs or beliefs that seem strange to us since they are so far removed from twentieth-century culture.

For example, what were household gods and why did Rachel steal them from her father (Gen 31:19)? Why was Jonah so fearful of the Ninevites? Who were the Samaritans, and why was there such hatred between them and the Jews (Jn 4:9)? What was the city of Corinth like, and what special temptations did the Corinthians face because they lived there? As we come to understand the answers to such questions, we receive new insight into how God's Word applied to their particular actions, fears, conflicts and temptations.

Imagine we are studying Amos, and we come across the following verse: "On the day I punish Israel for her sins . . . the horns of the altar will be cut off and fall to the ground" (Amos 3:14). This verse is meaningless to us in the twentieth century, but a Bible dictionary or encyclopedia will help us understand what Amos meant.

If we look up the word *altar* or *horn,* we discover that the altar in the temple had horn-shaped projections at each of its four corners. The sacrificial blood was smeared on these. In Old Testament times, many Jews believed the altar was a place of refuge. Those seeking safety would run to the temple and grab the horns of the altar. Amos is warning that the Israelites will flee to the altar and find its horns (that is, its protection) are gone!

We can also discover a great deal about the culture simply from the book or passage being studied. For example, the Gospels are full of references to life in first-century Palestine. We know that the Jews were under Roman rule (Lk 3:1) and expected the Messiah to come and free them from their enemies (Lk 1:71). We read about the legalism and externalism of the religious authorities and how they hindered a true knowledge of God (Mt 23). We also gain an understanding of everyday life in Bible times: business practices (Lk 16:1-18), weddings (Jn 2), funerals (Jn 11), wages (Mt 20:1-16), taxes (Mt 22:15-22) and so on. It is impossible to study the Bible without becoming immersed in ancient Middle Eastern culture. As we become more familiar with that culture, we are better able to cross this barrier between our world and theirs.

Crossing the geographical barrier. Some people are fortunate enough to visit the Holy Land. When they return, they report that the Bible comes to life in ways they have never experienced before. Those of us who have not visited the Holy Land can also have this experience in a more limited way. As we learn about biblical geography, many Bible passages take on new meaning.

For example, in Amos 1:3—2:16 the prophet condemns Damascus, Gaza, Tyre, Edom, Ammon, Moab, Judah and Israel. At first it may seem that Amos mentions these cities and nations at random, but a closer examination reveals otherwise. The first three are the capitals of heathen nations unrelated to Israel. The next three are blood relatives of Israel. Judah, the seventh, is Israel's brother nation to the south. Finally, Israel itself is named.

The effect on Amos's audience would have been staggering. The Israelites would have cheered at his judgments against the heathen nations. But as his words came closer and closer to home—Ammon, Moab, Judah—they would have begun to sweat. With the words "For three sins of Israel, even for four, I will not turn back my wrath," they were caught in Amos's coil of condemnation.

There are several ways to become familiar with biblical geography. Many Bibles include maps for the reader to consult. A good Bible atlas or a Bible dictionary can also supply valuable information about unfamiliar places.[3] These sources can help us trace the route of the Exodus, show us the cities conquered by Joshua and identify Israel's neighboring enemies. They can allow us to follow the ministry of Jesus and the missionary journeys of Paul. We can learn the location of the New Testament churches and how their setting may have influenced their life and culture. If we consult these sources whenever we come across an unfamiliar location in the Bible, they can help us cross the geographical barrier.

Learning to Read

Imagine that you have entered the time machine and have completely crossed the barriers of time, language, culture and geography. You are in Corinth in the first century. You are dressed in Greek clothes. You speak Greek fluently and know the surrounding culture and geography. You are even a regular visitor in the church at Corinth and are intimately acquainted with the people and problems in the church.

As you are gathering for worship in a nearby home, a messenger comes to the door with a letter from Paul, the letter we now call 1 Corinthians. You unroll the scroll and begin reading the letter (in Greek, of course!). Does the fact that you have successfully crossed the barriers of time, language, culture and geography mean that you will automatically understand what Paul is saying to the Corinthians? Not necessarily.

The apostle Peter was one of Paul's contemporaries and still found some things in his letters "hard to understand" (2 Pet 3:16). Of course Peter's difficulty may have been that Paul was unclear in places. But even when Paul writes clearly, our success in understanding him (or any other author) will depend on how skillful we are at reading. One aspect, therefore, of learning how to study the Bible focuses on acquiring reading skills—the kind of skills that will help us whether we are reading the Bible, a novel, a magazine or a newspaper.

Several years ago the *New York Times* ran an advertisement of Mortimer Adler's *How to Read a Book*. Under the picture of a puzzled adolescent reading a letter were these words:

How to Read a Love Letter

This young man has just received his first love letter. He may have read it three or four times, but he is just beginning. To read it as accurately as he would like, would require several dictionaries and a good deal of close work with a few experts of etymology and philology. However, he will do all right without them.

He will ponder over the exact shade of meaning of every word, every comma. She has headed the letter, "Dear John." What, he asks himself, is the exact significance of those words? Did she refrain from saying "Dearest" because she was bashful? Would "My Dear" have sounded too formal? Jeepers, maybe she would have said "Dear So-and-So" to anybody! A worried frown will now appear on his face. But it disappears as soon as he really gets to thinking about the first sentence. She certainly wouldn't have written *that* to anybody!

And so he works his way through the letter, one moment perched blissfully on a cloud, the next moment huddled miserably behind an eight-ball. It has started a hundred questions in his mind. He could quote it by heart. In fact, he will—to himself—for weeks to come.

The advertisement concludes: "If people read books with anything like the same concentration, we'd be a race of mental giants."[4]

The Bible is God's love letter to us. If we want to understand its meaning, we must read with the eagerness and intensity of the young man in the advertisement.

As we read, our first goal is to answer one primary question: What did the author mean to convey to the original readers? (The question of what the passage means to us today will be covered in later chapters.)

You can discover the meaning of the author by following five guidelines:

1. Identify the type of literature you are studying. A cult expert was giving a lecture one evening on Mormonism. A few Mor-

mons heard about the lecture and decided to attend. About half-
way through the meeting, one of them stood up and began
arguing that God the Father has a physical body like ours. He
"proved" his point by quoting passages which refer to God's
"right arm," "hand," "eyes" and so on. The cult expert asked him
to read aloud Psalm 17:8: "Hide me in the shadow of your
wings."

"But that is simply a figure of speech," protested the Mormon.

"Exactly!" replied the speaker.

The biblical authors communicated in a variety of ways—
through stories, letters, poems, proverbs, parables, metaphors
and symbols. Each type of literature has its own unique features.
We must identify the type of literature and language an author
is using in order to interpret his meaning correctly. If we assume
he is speaking literally when he is speaking metaphorically (the
mistake made by the Mormon), we end up with nonsense.

A Bible dictionary can help you identify the type of literature
you are studying. For example, if you are studying the Psalms,
it would be wise to read an article on Hebrew poetry in order
to learn how it differs from modern poetry. Likewise, if you are
studying Revelation, read an article on apocalyptic literature. It
will explain why this kind of literature seems so strange to us and
will offer suggestions for interpreting it correctly.[5]

2. Get an overview of the book. On a windswept plain in Peru,
archaeologists discovered a vast series of strange lines covering
an area thirty-seven miles long. They first thought these lines
were ancient roads. Their larger significance was not discovered
until the men flew over the area. The lines joined to form de-
signs, immense murals of insects, birds, fish and geometric
shapes that could only be seen from high above.

An overview helps us discover the meaning of an author in two ways. First, it enables us to discover the main *theme* of the book as we observe repeated ideas. Second, an overview helps us discover the *structure* of the book—how the parts of the book contribute to the overall theme.

An overview is like looking through a zoom lens. Begin with a panoramic view through the lens by reading quickly through the book, trying to discover repeated ideas or words that tie the book together. When it isn't possible to read the entire book, skim through its contents, paying particular attention to chapter or paragraph headings in your Bible.

Next, zoom in closer by looking for major sections or divisions within the book. Each section will focus primarily on one subject. Once you have discovered that subject, try to summarize it by briefly titling the section. Now you are ready to focus on the details of the landscape—the paragraphs, sentences and words.

3. Study the book passage by passage.

Once you have an overview of the theme and structure of a book, begin studying it passage by passage. In our modern Bibles a passage can be a paragraph, a group of paragraphs or a chapter. Realize, however, that the Bible did not originally contain chapters, paragraphs or verses (or even punctuation!). These are helpful additions to our Bibles, but we need not be bound by them.

4. Be sensitive to the mood of the book or passage. The Bible is more than a collection of ideas. The biblical authors and characters were people like us with passions and feelings. Sorrow and agony permeate Jesus' experience in Gethsemane. Galatians radiates the heat of Paul's anger toward the Judaizers and his perplexity over the Galatians. Psalm 148 is bursting with praise.

While this is a more subjective aspect of Bible study, it can give us rich insights into the feelings and motivations of the biblical authors or characters. This in turn will add depth to our understanding of what they are saying.

5. *Compare your interpretation with one or two commentaries.* Once you feel you have understood the main subject of the passage and what the author is saying about it, compare your interpretation with that of one or two good commentaries.[6] They can give you additional insights which you might have missed and can serve as a corrective if you have misunderstood something that the author has said. But do your best to understand the passage on your own before consulting commentaries.

Returning to the Present

Now we are ready to re-enter the time machine and return to the twentieth century. As we travel from the biblical world back to our own, we must *recross* the barriers of time, culture, language and geography.

In the broadest sense, this is what application is all about. We seek to apply what we learned in Jerusalem, Ephesus or Corinth to our present-day needs in Chicago, Los Angeles or London. We take the message originally spoken in Greek, Hebrew and Aramaic and communicate it clearly in our own language. We take the eternal truths originally spoken in a different time and culture and apply them to the similar-yet-different needs of our own culture.

One important step in preparing to make this return journey is to find general principles which underlie the specific situations and commands of Scripture. How we do this is the subject of the next chapter.

CHAPTER FOUR

STEP TWO: FINDING GENERAL PRINCIPLES

*A*s *a large family gathered around the table for meals, each* member took a turn saying grace. Everyone, however, dreaded the meals when the youngest presided.

Grace seemed like an endless ordeal because the boy's prayers were so specific. He would begin with the contents of his own plate and then work his way around the table: "Dear Lord, thank you for my egg, Mommy's egg, Daddy's egg, Stephen's egg and Lucy's egg. Thank you for my bacon, Mommy's bacon, Daddy's bacon, Stephen's bacon and Lucy's bacon. Thank you for my toast, Mommy's toast, Daddy's toast, Stephen's toast and Lucy's toast. Thank you for my orange juice, Mommy's orange juice, Daddy's orange juice [tedious, isn't it!], Stephen's orange juice and Lucy's orange juice," and so on until he had named each item they were eating. Then he would conclude his lengthy prayer by mentioning whatever remained on the table: "Thank you for the salt, thank you for the pepper, thank you for the butter and thank you for the jelly. In Jesus' name, Amen." At that point everyone would breathe a sigh of relief and begin the now-cold meal.

As the boy grew a little older, however, one morning he surprised everyone. The usual, awful moment had arrived. The other family members bowed their heads, folded their hands and bit their lips. They all knew it would be at least five or ten minutes before they could taste the hickory-smoked bacon and the golden pancakes or drink their orange juice and the once-hot coffee. The youngest began as usual, but astonished everyone by saying, "Dear Lord, thank you for this food. In Jesus' name, Amen." He had learned to generalize!

Learning to generalize is one of the most important steps in applying the Bible. When, on the surface, a passage seems to have little application to our situation today, we need to look beneath the surface for a general principle.

The Greatest Commandment
The idea of finding general principles behind the specific teachings of Scripture is not a recent discovery. Jesus himself taught us to do this.

An expert in the Law once came to Jesus in order to test his knowledge of Scripture. "Teacher," he asked, "which is the greatest commandment in the Law?" In asking this question, the expert was inviting Jesus to comment on one of the most important issues of his day. The Jewish rabbis counted 613 individual commandments in the Law, regulating everything from mildewed clothing to sacrifices on the Day of Atonement. They tried to differentiate between "heavy" (or "great") commands and those which were "light" (or "little").[1]

The point, of course, was not to disregard the lesser commands in favor of the greater ones. Rather, they wondered whether some commands were greater in the sense that by obeying them a person automatically obeyed the lesser ones.

Jesus replied, " 'Love the Lord your God with all your heart and with all your soul and with all your mind.' This is the first and greatest commandment. And the second is like it: 'Love your neighbor as yourself.' " Notice especially what he said next: "*All the Law and the Prophets hang on these two commandments*" (Mt 22:36-40, emphasis mine).

In other words, the six hundred commandments could be summarized by just two. These two commandments were so general that they could apply to many different situations—in fact, they could apply to *every* situation. They expressed the inner motive and ultimate goal of every law given by God.[2]

Why then were the 600 commands necessary? They were needed to define and illustrate the general commands about love in the specific situations of everyday life. For example, what did it mean to love your neighbor in business practices? "Do not use dishonest standards when measuring length, weight or quantity" (Lev 19:35). What did it mean to love those who were hungry and needy? "When you reap the harvest of your land, do not reap to the very edges of your field or gather the gleanings of your harvest. . . . Leave them for the poor and the alien" (Lev 19:9-10).

In one sense, then, finding general principles behind the specific commands of Scripture is easy. Whatever the command, whatever the situation, we know that they are expressions of love for God and neighbor.

Yet it would get pretty monotonous if these were the only general principles we ever discovered. Imagine having love as the one and only theme of every sermon, every Christian book, every Bible study! Fortunately, this is not the case.

Levels of Application

The Bible contains many levels of application. These levels are like a pyramid, with only two commands (love for God and neighbor) at the pinnacle and all other commands at various levels between the pinnacle and the base.

The principles near the top of the pyramid are fewer in number because they are more general and abstract. The commands nearer the base of the pyramid (such as "Do not muzzle your ox") are more numerous because they are more specific, detailed and concrete.

The commands near the base sometimes seem pointless or obscure until we move up to higher levels on the pyramid to discover the principles or reasons for the commands. Conversely, the principles near the top of the pyramid often seem vague and abstract until they are fleshed out by the more concrete principles near the base.

Let's look at a passage that illustrates various levels of application.

Paul's instructions about food sacrificed to idols. In 1 Corinthians 8 Paul gives instructions about a subject which is seemingly irrelevant today—food sacrificed to idols. However, when we look more closely at the passage we discover that the issue of food is only one level of application, the one at the bottom of the pyramid. There are two other levels in the pyramid, each of which can be applied today.

Before we can look for these general principles, we must first understand the problem faced by Paul's readers and how the passage applied to them. Why were they concerned about food sacrificed to idols? The *Handbook of Life in Bible Times* helps us cross this cultural barrier:

> Even the relatively ordinary household duties of buying meat from the butcher or going out to dinner with friends were fraught with problems. Some butchers bought their produce wholesale from the pagan temples where it had been ritually slaughtered or partially offered as a sacrifice to idols. Christians in Corinth were unsure whether or not to buy such meat, or to eat it if it was set in front of them.[3]

Paul helps the Corinthians to see this problem from a biblical perspective. He tells them that in one sense he doesn't care whether they eat food sacrificed to idols. Why? First, he knows that there is really only one God: "We know that an idol is nothing at all in the world and that there is no God but one. For even if there are so-called gods, whether in heaven or on earth (as indeed there are many 'gods' and many 'lords'), yet for us there is but one God" (1 Cor 8:4-5). Second, Paul realizes that food is spiritually neutral: "Food does not bring us near to God; we are no worse if we do not eat, and no better if we do" (v. 8).

Yet Paul realizes that "not everyone knows this" (v. 7). Some Christians who had been deeply involved in idol worship might misunderstand if Paul and others ate food sacrificed to idols:

> For if anyone with a weak conscience sees you who have this

knowledge eating in an idol's temple, won't he be emboldened to eat what has been sacrificed to idols? So this weak brother, for whom Christ died, is destroyed by your knowledge. When you sin against your brothers in this way and wound their weak conscience, you sin against Christ. (vv. 10-12)

Rather than take this risk, Paul concludes: "Therefore, if what I eat causes my brother to fall into sin, I will never eat [idol] meat again, so that I will not cause him to fall" (v. 13).

Although Paul's conclusion not to eat idol meat has little application today, the reasons he gives are still valid. In verses 8-9 he states that the real issue isn't idol meat but rather "that the exercise of [our] freedom does not become a stumbling block to the weak." In other words, there is a more important principle at stake: Paul doesn't want us to do anything that might cause other Christians to sin by violating their consciences (vv. 7, 10). This would "wound" or "destroy" the persons, whereas Paul wants us to build them up in love (v. 1). This principle could apply to many questionable practices today.[4]

So we have moved from the very specific and irrelevant command about food sacrificed to idols to the more general and more applicable principle about not letting our freedom cause someone else to sin. Paul has even mentioned one of the two general principles behind this and every command of Scripture—that of building up our brother or sister through love (v. 1). Therefore, our pyramid in this passage has three levels of application:

Level 1 (the most specific): The Corinthians should not eat food sacrificed to idols if it causes those with weak consciences to follow their example.

Level 2 (more general): The Corinthians should not allow

their freedom (in any area) to become a stumbling block to the weak.

Level 3 (the most general): The Corinthians should only do those things which build up others in love.

If we realize that *every* passage of Scripture is part of the larger biblical pyramid with its various levels, applying the Bible becomes much easier. If a passage appears too specific to apply to our situation, we simply move up a level, looking for a general principle that we can apply.

Finding General Principles

Finding general principles in a passage is usually the result of asking the right questions. There are three important questions to ask, especially if the passage doesn't directly apply today:

Question 1: Does the author state a general principle? The passage in 1 Corinthians 8 illustrates the first and easiest way to find a general principle: simply look to see whether the author states that principle, as Paul did in verse 9. New Testament writers often state a general principle and then give several examples of how that principle applies to specific situations. Not all of the specifics will apply to us today, but the general principle will almost always apply.

For example, in Ephesians 6:5 Paul tells slaves, "Obey your earthly masters." Since slavery has been abolished for many years, this verse no longer has any *direct* application today. However, it is only one of three examples Paul gives the Ephesians. The other two are "Children, obey your parents in the Lord" (6:1) and "Wives, submit to your husbands as to the Lord" (5:22). Each of these examples illustrates the general principle, "Submit to one another out of reverence for Christ" (5:21).

Question 2: Why was this specific command or instruction given?
Whether an author states a general principle or not, we can
usually find one by looking not only at the command itself but
also at the *reason* for the command. Biblical commands are never
given at random but are always an expression of a higher level
in the pyramid. When we discover why a command is given, we
are able to move up one or more levels in the pyramid to a
principle that is applicable today.

The book of Galatians illustrates this approach. In Galatians
Paul gives his readers a very specific warning against circumcision. "Mark my words! I, Paul, tell you that if you let yourselves
be circumcised, Christ will be of no value to you at all. Again
I declare to every man who lets himself be circumcised that he
is obligated to obey the whole law" (Gal 5:2-3).

At face value these verses strictly forbid circumcision. They
also warn of serious consequences for those who allow themselves to be circumcised. Why, then, have some Christians
throughout the centuries continued to practice circumcision?
Have they simply been disobedient to Paul's command? The only
way to answer that question is to ask *why* Paul warned the Galatians against being circumcised.

If we look more closely at the passage, we see that the issue
was not the mere physical act of circumcision. How do we know
this? Because Paul tells the Galatians that "in Christ Jesus neither circumcision nor uncircumcision has any value" (v. 6). In
other words, it wasn't the physical act of circumcision Paul objected to but rather the *reason* for the circumcision. Paul states
that reason in verse 4: "You . . . are trying to be justified by law."

The Galatians were trying to be justified by keeping the law
of Moses, and circumcision was merely the outward expression

of this, their initiation into the Old Covenant. The *New Bible Dictionary* gives us further insight into the controversy over circumcision:

> The "churches of Galatia" had evidently been visited by Judaizers who cast doubt on Paul's apostolic status and insisted that . . . it was necessary to be circumcised and to conform in other respects to the Jewish law in order to attain salvation. . . . The Judaizers justified their insistence on circumcision by appealing to the example of Abraham: since circumcision was the seal of God's covenant with him, they argued, no uncircumcised person could have a share in that covenant with all the blessings which went with it.[5]

So we have moved up a level from the very specific warning, "Do not let yourself be circumcised," to the more general command, "Do not seek to be justified by law." This is a step in the right direction, but we are still somewhat short of a timeless principle. Few people today are tempted to keep the law of Moses—to offer sacrifices, to observe feasts or festivals or ceremonial washings—the kinds of things the Galatians were tempted to do. So again we must ask, *why* did Paul object to such practices? What was wrong with trying to be justified by law?

The answer, fortunately, is not difficult to find. In Galatians 3 Paul asks the Galatians why, after believing the gospel and receiving the Spirit, they are turning from grace to another method of salvation. Only this time he doesn't just speak of their trying to obey the law but rather asks, "Are you now trying to attain your goal by human effort?" (Gal 3:3).

This is the answer we have been looking for, the ultimate reason Paul objected to circumcision and law-keeping. The Galatians were tempted to trust in *human effort* rather than in Jesus

Christ. This general principle is repeated throughout Galatians and is the foundation of Paul's argument: We cannot earn God's acceptance by human effort but must receive it by faith. This principle transcends the specific situation faced by the Galatians—circumcision and law-keeping—and is as applicable in the twentieth century as it was in the first.

This passage also reinforces the idea that we may have to move up more than one level in our pyramid in order to find a general principle that is applicable today. Our pyramid in this passage looks like this:

Level 1: The Galatians should not seek to be circumcised. Why?

Level 2: Because no one can be justified by keeping the law. Why?

Level 3: Because we cannot earn God's acceptance by human effort but must accept it by faith.

By looking for the reason behind Paul's command in level one, we discovered the general principle stated in level two. Yet this principle was still too specific to Jewish culture to be applicable today. So by again asking why Paul made the statement in level two, we found the general principle in level three. This principle is broad enough to apply to situations we face.

Question 3: Does the broader context reveal a general principle? As we look for general principles, it is extremely important to consider not only the immediate but also the broader context of a passage. For example, in 1 Corinthians 8 it was a simple matter to find Paul's general principle, since he stated it in the immediate context (v. 9). In Ephesians, however, it was necessary to look at the three paragraphs preceding Paul's discussion of slavery in order to see his other examples of the principle "submit to one another out of reverence for Christ" (5:21). In Galatians we were able to discover one general principle in the immediate context (level two in the pyramid), but the broader and more applicable principle (level three) only came to light by searching the earlier chapters. Ultimately, the entire Bible provides the context and guiding principles for every passage within it.

Principles and Proof-texts

One day I overheard two seminary students studying for their senior theology exam. This exam was to be the culmination of their seminary experience, the high point of four years of diligent study and spiritual growth. It should have revealed their ability to think through complex issues from a biblical perspective.

Yet what I heard amazed me. One student said to the other. "Give me a verse on the filling of the Holy Spirit."

"Ephesians 5:18," the other replied.

"What about a verse on the eternal security of the believer?" he asked.

"Philippians 1:6!"

"Tell me a verse which proves the sinfulness of humanity," he demanded.

"Romans 3:23," the other shot back, faster than I could blink my ever-widening eyes.

They went on like this for over an hour, drilling each other, asking questions, and responding with verses for every conceivable subject. I couldn't believe what I was hearing. This wasn't senior theology; it was a Scripture-memory quiz, the theological equivalent of baby talk!

John Stott writes: "The truly Christian mind has repented of 'proof-texting' (the notion that we can settle every doctrinal and ethical issue by quoting a single, isolated text, whereas God has given us a comprehensive revelation), and instead saturates itself in the whole of Scripture."[6]

Finding general principles in Scripture is not the same as looking for proof-texts. Neither is it an attempt to tie up the truths of Scripture into neat little propositional packages. Rather, we look beyond the specific commands, examples and promises of Scripture in order to seek the mind and heart of God. We want to grasp not only *what* God said (although that is extremely important) but also *why* he said it. Our passion is to develop a godly mindset, a world view that is shaped by the broad scope of Scripture.

Stott goes on to say:

"There is a . . . better and more Christian way to approach today's complicated questions: develop a Christian mind, namely a mind which has firmly grasped the basic presuppositions of Scripture and is thoroughly informed with biblical truth. Only such a mind can think with Christian integrity about the problems of the contemporary world.[7]

As we look for biblical principles, we are seeking to feel God's heartbeat in the verses, paragraphs, chapters and books of Scripture. With the help of the Holy Spirit, our goal is nothing less than to discern the mind of God.

Almost, But Not Quite

Several years ago some seminary students were asked to preach a sermon on the parable of the Good Samaritan. Each student was deliberately delayed until moments before his sermon was to begin. As each one raced frantically across campus with text in hand, he was met by someone posing as a person in need. Ironically, not one of them stopped to help the person—they had an important sermon to preach!

This chapter has tried to provide both a framework for thinking about general principles and a simple method for discovering them. However, a general principle can simply be a pious platitude unless we take one more vital step: we must seek to apply that principle to the situations we face today. How we do this is the subject of the next chapter.

STEP THREE: APPLYING GENERAL PRINCIPLES TODAY

*I*n the movie The Gods Must Be Crazy, *a Coke bottle is thrown* from an airplane and lands in a tiny community of African bush people. Because it dropped from the sky, they think the bottle is a gift from the gods.

At first this isolated tribe is puzzled by the bottle's strange appearance. They have never seen glass before, not to mention a bottle. What is this thing good for? Yet after a while they begin to find many uses for the Coke bottle. Because of its hardness, it makes an excellent hammer for smashing roots. Because it is cylindrical, the bottle can be used as a rolling pin. They find it can even be used as a musical instrument if they blow into the opening. The more they think about it, the more uses they discover for the bottle.

In one sense, a biblical principle is like that Coke bottle. We know the principle is a gift from God—even if the Coke bottle isn't. But at first we don't know quite what to do with it. Its usefulness only becomes apparent as we think about how it can affect our lives.

Yet it is precisely at this point that many people fail to apply the Bible. Some simply don't take the time to reflect on how the principle might apply to the situations they face. Others make the opposite mistake of applying the principle to situations for which it was never intended. Like the bush people, they use a biblical "Coke bottle" as a rolling pin!

This chapter will provide guidelines for properly applying the principles we discover in Scripture.

Keep My Commandments

In the previous chapter we saw that Jesus looked for general principles behind the hundreds of specific commands in Scripture. He taught that love for God and neighbor summarizes "all the Law and the Prophets" (Mt 22:36-40). In a culture absorbed with the minute details of Scripture, Jesus told the "expert in the law" to look for the big picture, the principles behind the Law. In other words, he encouraged him to move his eyes from the base of the pyramid to the pinnacle.

However, it would be wrong to assume that Jesus did not care about the specific commands in Scripture. Just before he went to the cross, he told his disciples: "If you love me, you will keep My commandments" (Jn 14:15, NASB). Later in the same passage, he put it another way: "Whoever has my commands and obeys them, he is the one who loves me" (v. 21). The apostle

John, who was present on this occasion, commented years later: "This is love for God: to obey his commands. And his commands are not burdensome" (1 Jn 5:3).

In other words, just as Jesus urged the expert in the law to move his eyes from the base of the pyramid to the pinnacle, so he urged his disciples to move from the pinnacle back down to the base. It isn't sufficient to love God or our neighbor in the abstract. Our love must be expressed in specific and concrete ways. Just as love is behind every command in Scripture, so the converse is also true: every command in Scripture is a specific way of expressing our love for God and our neighbor.

In fact, the general principles we discover in Scripture are inseparable from the specific commands. For example, it is impossible to love someone without expressing that love through patience, kindness, generosity and so on. Likewise, it is impossible to be generous (or patient or kind) to someone without doing so in specific ways, such as giving the person food, money, clothing or something else he or she needs. Our love and our generosity are never really expressed until they reach this tangible level.

Therefore, after we discover a general principle in Scripture by moving up one or more levels in the pyramid, we must move back down the pyramid—all the way to the base! In other words, having discovered a principle behind the situation faced by those in Scripture, we must now apply that principle to situations we face today.

Applying General Principles

As we seek to apply a general principle to our lives, we have three options: (1) we can apply the principle to the *identical* situation faced by those in the passage; (2) we can apply it to a *comparable* situation; (3) we can apply it to an entirely *different* situation, depending on what we mean by *different*.

Applying a principle to the identical situation. As we read the Bible, there will be times when the situation faced by the original readers is identical to our own. For example, in Ephesians 6 Paul tells his readers to "put on the full armor of God so that you can take your stand against the devil's schemes. For our struggle is not against flesh and blood, but against . . . the powers of this dark world and against the spiritual forces of evil in the heavenly realms" (vv. 11-12). Although Paul's command is couched in the language of the first century (the imagery of Roman armor), his exhortation is as vital today as it was then. Why? Because the ultimate nature of our battle has not changed in two thousand years. We still struggle against demonic forces, and our only defense is the power of God.

Likewise, when the author of Hebrews tells his readers, "Keep your lives free from the love of money and be content with what you have" (Heb 13:5), we know his words transcend the barriers of time. Money has always been an object of passion and allure. Undoubtedly, people in every age have asked, "How much is enough? Just a little bit more!"

In both passages we begin and end on level one of the pyramid. Because our situations are identical to those faced by the original audience, God's Word to us is the same as it was to them.

Applying a principle to a comparable situation. Quite often, however, our situation is not identical to that of the original readers. In such cases we must move up a level in the pyramid, looking for a general principle we can apply to a *comparable* situation.

Our situation must be truly comparable to the original situation in order for the principle to apply. For example, the principle behind Paul's command against eating food offered to idols was that we should "be careful . . . that the exercise of [our] freedom does not become a stumbling block to the weak" (1 Cor 8:9). Unfortunately, this passage and the one similar to it in Romans 14 have been used in ways that Paul never intended.

A few years ago many churches claimed that long hair, beards and guitars in church were sinful for Christians because they were a "stumbling block" to the older generation. However, they were trying to apply Paul's words to a situation that simply wasn't comparable to the one in Corinth or Rome. For Paul, a stumbling block was something that "causes my brother to fall into sin" (v. 13). For the older generation, a "stumbling block" was something offensive or distasteful. Likewise, for Paul a "weak brother" was someone who was tempted to imitate the behavior of those who ate idol meat. But I seriously doubt that the older generation was tempted to grow beards or long hair.

On the other hand, Christians may be correct in applying the "stumbling block" principle to the practice of drinking alcoholic beverages. If my "freedom" to drink might tempt a former alcoholic to resume a practice he cannot control, I should give up that freedom. Likewise, if my freedom to go to certain kinds of movies tempts someone who feels such movies are wrong, then I should care more about my brother than about my freedom. Both of these situations are comparable to the issue of eating food sacrificed to idols.

How can we know whether our situation is truly comparable to one in Scripture? First, we must identify the *key elements* which are common to both the original situation and the principle we wish to apply. Then we must determine whether our situation contains each of these key elements.

For example, both the principle and the situation mentioned in 1 Corinthians 8 have three key elements in common: (1) my freedom; (2) a stumbling block; and (3) a weak brother or sister. None of these elements could be omitted from 1 Corinthians 8 without losing something essential to Paul's meaning.

Superficially, the first illustration mentioned earlier seemed to contain these three elements: (1) the freedom to wear long hair or grow a beard; (2) the stumbling block of offending the older generation; and (3) the weaker brothers and sisters who were offended. However, as I mentioned previously, the second and third elements really weren't comparable to those described in the principle or embodied in the original situation. Therefore, the principle could not legitimately be applied to that situation.

On the other hand, the second illustration contained all three elements in a way that was truly comparable: (1) the freedom of drinking alcoholic beverages or going to certain kinds of movies; (2) the stumbling block of causing someone to sin by violating his or her conscience; and (3) the weaker person who feels it is wrong to drink or go to certain kinds of movies. The principle in 1 Corinthians 8 legitimately applies to that situation.

When you try to identify the key elements in a general principle, the original situation and a contemporary situation, it is helpful to look at them together. First, briefly summarize the issue in the original situation. Next, write down the general principle behind that situation. Then compare the two, looking for how the elements were expressed in the original situation. Finally, you must ask whether your contemporary situation contains those elements.

For example, consider Peter's simple command to slaves in 1 Peter 2:18: "Slaves, submit yourselves to your masters with all respect, not only to those who are good and considerate, but also to those who are harsh." Because we are unable to apply this command directly, we must move up a level in the pyramid, looking for the general principle behind the command. Fortunately, Peter states that principle a few verses earlier: "Submit yourselves for the Lord's sake to every authority instituted among men: whether to the king, as the supreme authority, or to governors, who are sent by him to punish those who do wrong and to commend those who do right" (vv. 13-14).

In other words, the situation of slaves submitting to masters is just one example of the general principle "Submit yourselves for the Lord's sake to every authority." Peter also gives other examples of those in authority over his readers, mentioning kings, governors and husbands (3:1). In each case, his readers are to submit to these authorities "for the Lord's sake" (2:13).

We might summarize the original situation (slaves submitting to masters) and the general principle (all Christians submitting to those in authority) as follows:

Original situation: Slaves should submit to their masters [for the Lord's sake].

General principle: Christians should submit to those in authority over them for the Lord's sake.

When viewed together, it is easy to see which key elements the two statements have in common and which elements are variables which change from one situation to another. Obviously, one key element is submission, since the word *submit* appears in both statements. Likewise, in both statements there is someone who has authority and someone who is under authority. Although the statement *for the Lord's sake* does not occur in both places, Peter's earlier statement makes it clear that this is the ultimate motive for submitting to those in authority over us.

These key elements are an essential part of both the original statement and the general principle behind that statement. If we were to omit any of these key elements, we would lose some of the force and meaning contained in Peter's command.

On the other hand, *slaves* and *masters* are clearly variables which change from situation to situation. We might substitute *subjects* and *kings, citizens* and *governors,* or *wives* and *husbands* as Peter suggests. Or, as we seek to make contemporary applications of the general principle, we might substitute modern equivalents of those in authority over us: presidents, prime ministers, mayors and so on. We might, for example, make the following contemporary statement:

Personal application: As a Christian, I should submit to my supervisor for the Lord's sake.

Because this statement shares each of the key elements with the general principle and the original situation, it is a valid application of Peter's command. The key elements not only help us to find comparable situations today but also become safeguards against applying Scripture in ways God never intended.[1]

Most of the applications we make from Scripture will be comparable, rather than identical, to the original situation. The Lord never intended to cover every possible situation in the Bible. Rather, by giving us general principles behind the specific situations in Scripture, he provided us with means for applying his Word to a wide variety of circumstances.

Applying a principle to a different situation. Is it ever possible to apply a principle to a situation that is entirely different from the original one? That depends on what we mean by *different*.

A contemporary situation must always be comparable to the original situation in one respect: both must share the same key elements found in the general principle. If we omit one or more of these key elements—as in the case of long hair, beards and guitars mentioned previously—we are no longer really applying the principle found in the passage.

We must realize, however, that the original situation and the contemporary situation are comparable only in the sense that they both contain the key elements found in the general principle. Beyond that, the two situations may be very different. This is a simple but important point to remember. When we are looking for contemporary situations that are comparable to those in Scripture, we only need to be concerned about the key elements, not the superficial resemblance—or lack of resemblance—between our situation and the original one.

Let me illustrate what I am saying. A few years ago our Sunday-school class was studying Galatians 4:9-11. In that passage Paul expressed concern that the Galatians were turning back to practices they left behind when they became Christians:

But now that you know God—or rather are known by God— how is it that you are turning back to those weak and miserable principles? Do you wish to be enslaved by them all over again? You are observing special days and months and seasons and years! I fear for you, that somehow I have wasted my efforts on you.

Our Sunday-school teacher asked the class whether we were guilty of observing special days and months and seasons and years. Yet instead of getting us to admit our guilt and forsake such practices, his question backfired. Various members of the class began to express a need for such special days. They said their spiritual lives needed more structure and discipline. They welcomed a chance to set aside special times for prayer, Bible study or worship. Superficially, at least, they seemed to desire the very thing Paul warned against!

After the class, I thought about what had gone wrong with the teacher's question. It seemed to me that he had failed to "connect" with the class and with the passage in at least three important ways.

First, he had failed to explain the original situation in the passage. The "special days and months and seasons and years" were probably part of the Jewish calendar. The Galatians thought that, like circumcision, the Jewish holidays and celebrations would make them more acceptable to God.

In contrast, Paul realized that any attempt to earn God's acceptance would result in slavery to a worthless list of do's and don'ts. The Galatians didn't need to earn God's acceptance because they were already accepted in Christ. Likewise, they didn't need to act like slaves because they were God's children and his heirs (v. 7).

In light of the above, the original situation might be summarized as follows:

Original situation: By observing Jewish holidays in hope of gaining God's favor, the Galatians were acting more like slaves than sons of God. Such practices would not make them more acceptable to God but would merely enslave them.

Second, our teacher had failed to identify the general principle behind Paul's command to the Galatians. A careful reading of the passage reveals that Paul wants them to act like sons rather than slaves. In the broader context of the letter, he also warns them against trying to earn God's acceptance because they are already acceptable in Christ.

Therefore, the general principle might be summarized as follows:

General principle: We should act like children of God rather than slaves. That means we shouldn't do anything to try to earn God's acceptance. When done for that reason, religious practices merely enslave us.

Finally, our teacher had assumed that observing special days, months, seasons and years was a key element in the passage. In fact, however, it was a variable which might change from situation to situation. As our class realized, there is nothing inherently wrong with observing special days and months and seasons and years. Under certain circumstances, such practices may even be pleasing to the Lord. Paul himself had said in Romans 14:5-6: "One man considers one day more sacred than another; another man considers every day alike. Each one should be fully convinced in his own mind. He who regards one day as special, does so to the Lord."

The key elements—those common to both the original situation and the general principle—have to do with (1) certain *practices* (2) which are done in order to *earn God's acceptance* (3) but which in reality *enslave us.*

Certainly Christians today—including those in our Sunday-school class—sometimes act more like slaves than children of God. But we do so in ways that are very different from the Galatians. Our class simply wasn't threatened by the danger of "days and months and seasons and years." We usually try to earn God's acceptance through other means.

For example, in our performance-oriented culture we might

feel that God loves and accepts us more if we have a quiet time each day or witness on a regular basis or give a certain amount of money. When we sin, we may feel unacceptable until we go a few days without repeating that particular sin. In subtle but real ways we assume God's acceptance is based on what we do rather than on what Christ has done. Just as the Galatians did, we become enslaved by practices which arise out of a warped theology. On the surface the issues look very different from those faced two thousand years ago. But underneath they violate the same general principle Paul wrote about in Galatians.

The Missing Ingredient

At times, the process of finding and applying biblical principles may seem more mechanical than spiritual. After all, where does God fit into this process? Has he merely left us with a set of principles to discover and obey, while he has gone away to Acapulco?

If that were the case, then the Pharisees would have been right. True religion would merely involve the scrupulous observance of 613 commands rather than a vital and living *relationship* with God. And eternal life would involve *doing* rather than *knowing*.

In fact, eternal life involves both doing and knowing. At the beginning of this chapter, I quoted Christ's statement: "Whoever has my commands and obeys them, he is the one who loves me" (Jn 14:21). The remainder of the verse supplies the ingredient which is missing from this discussion. Jesus goes on to say: "He who loves me will be loved by my Father, and I too will love him and show myself to him."

Love is the dominant force in our relationship with Jesus Christ. However, as in any relationship, love must be expressed.

Jesus wants us to express our love for him by obeying his commands. He, in turn, promises to express his love for us by revealing himself to us.

Our obedience, then, should be anything but dry and lifeless. It is a warm, affectionate, even passionate, means of showing Christ how much he means to us. We seek to understand and obey his Word in order to *please* him.

Yet we also seek to understand and obey his Word in order to *know* him. In the ongoing process of loving and obeying Jesus Christ, something astounding happens—he lovingly reveals himself to us, both in the pages of Scripture and in the innermost recesses of our hearts and lives. The result, as Bishop Ryle has written, is that "there is more of heaven on earth to be obtained than most Christians are aware of."[2]

This passionate knowledge of both Scripture and the Lord of Scripture will never come to those who merely analyze or dissect God's Word. Such knowledge is reserved for those who are willing to devote themselves to a discipline that has largely been abandoned today. That essential discipline is the subject of the next chapter.

CHAPTER SIX

THE
IMPORTANCE OF
MEDITATION

*T*he Greek mathematician Archimedes was once puzzling over a problem. He was trying to determine whether a crown supposedly made of pure gold actually contained a quantity of silver. Days passed without any sign of a solution. Then one day he visited the public baths. While he was immersed both in the bath and in thought, the answer came to him. He was so excited that he leaped out of the water and ran naked through the streets of the city, crying "Eureka! Eureka!" ("I've found it! I've found it!").

As Christians, we are often equally puzzled about application. We work hard at understanding the original situation. We diligently search for the principle expressed in the text. Then when we find it, we assume the process of application is complete, when in fact it has just begun! Like Archimedes, we need to immerse ourselves—not only in Scripture but also in thought and in prayer. Only then can we expect the insights needed to apply Scripture to the specific areas of our lives.

The great Baptist preacher Charles Spurgeon wrote: "Let us, dear brethren, try to *get saturated with the gospel*. I always find that I can preach best when I can manage to lie asoak in my text. I like to get a text, and find out its meaning and bearings, and so on; and then, after I have bathed in it, I delight to lie down in it, and let it soak into me."[1]

For the biblical writers, this process of soaking in a text and letting it soak into us was known as *meditation*. The psalmist writes:

> Blessed is the man who does not walk in the counsel of the wicked. . . . But his delight is in the law of the LORD, and on his law he *meditates* day and night. (Ps 1:1-2, emphasis mine)
>
> Oh, how I love your law! I *meditate* on it all day long. Your commands make me wiser than my enemies, for they are ever with me. I have more insight than all my teachers, for I *meditate* on your statutes. (Ps 119:97-99, emphasis mine)

"Day and night"? "All day long"? In our age of instant coffee and the fifteen-minute Quiet Time, such devotion to Scripture may seem quite foreign. But if the Bible is to have an impact on our lives, we must meditate both on the principles we discover and on how they relate to the situations we face each day.

Thought and Prayer

Effective meditation must be done both *thoughtfully* and *prayerfully*. In 2 Timothy 2:7 Paul writes to his young associate: "Think over what I say, for the Lord will grant you understanding in everything" (RSV). Notice the two halves of this verse.

"Think over what I say." Application requires careful thought. We must take the truths we have learned from Scripture and reflect on how they relate to our world. John Stott urges us to

> Read the text, reread it, and read it again. Turn it over and over in your mind, like Mary the mother of Jesus who wondered at all the things the shepherds had told her, "pondering them in her heart". (Luke 2:18, 19) Probe your text, like a bee with a spring blossom, or like a hummingbird probing a hibiscus flower for its nectar. Worry at it like a dog with a bone. Suck it as a child sucks an orange. Chew it as a cow chews the cud.[2]

As we meditate on Scripture, we need to think as broadly as possible. Begin with your personal life. How might the principle affect your relationship with God? How might it make a difference in your family or friendships? What affect should it have on your work, your leisure, your finances, your future?

For example, while writing this book I was studying 1 Corinthians 9, where Paul talks about his rights as an apostle. In the first part of the chapter, Paul focuses on his right to receive financial support—a right he chose not to exercise.

Not being an apostle myself, or someone who needed to raise financial support, I wasn't sure how these verses applied to me. However, after further thought and study I discovered a general principle which was common to chapters 8 and 9. Paul believed that *people* were more important than his rights and more important than his freedoms. That principle had real possibilities.

In fact, as I thought about how it might apply to my relationships, I began to get uncomfortable. During that time I had volunteered to be on a Christmas-party planning committee at work. Six other people also volunteered, and we began meeting weekly to plan the program.

We decided to do an adaptation of Dickens's *A Christmas Carol*, revising it to fit some of the people and situations at work. It seemed like a great idea until we actually began writing a script. I thought the script should follow the original story line, departing only when necessary. Another committee member thought we shouldn't worry about sticking closely to the story. He wanted the script to be contemporary and upbeat. One person thought we should have some kind of message in our play. Someone else said that would be too "preachy."

At every step of the way we argued and even fought over how the play should be done. I'm sure I stepped on more than a few toes. Feelings were hurt, and relationships began to be tense. I went to one woman and asked her how she felt about the situation. She said, "Everyone had told me how much fun it was to plan the Christmas party. I'm not having any fun at all. In fact, I don't even like coming to the meetings!"

As I thought about her comment, it occurred to me that I had come to care more about the script than about the people on the committee. In order to get my way, I was being insensitive to their feelings and opinions. I decided that no script was worth damaging my relationship with those I cared about. During the remainder of our time together, I worked hard at being more open and flexible—even if I disagreed with some of the decisions made.

Was the play ruined since other people's ideas were sometimes accepted instead of mine? Not at all! As it turned out, the script had elements of Dickens as well as original ideas. It had a subtle message that wasn't preachy. People loved the play and said it was one of the best Christmas programs in years.

I mention this incident because it illustrates why it is necessary to meditate on biblical principles. The principle I had learned about people and rights was nothing more than a principle until it "connected" with an actual situation I was facing. Only then did it have a personal impact on my life.

Unfortunately, many of us think only about our personal lives and in so doing blunt the full impact of Scripture. When you discover a biblical principle, be sure to ask broader questions as well. How might the principle affect your church or community? Does it have any ethical or social applications? What about economic or political implications? Just as the Bible originally spoke to each of these areas in ancient Israel and Rome, so we need to allow biblical principles to become incarnate in twentieth-century life and culture. Meditation is one of the keys for achieving that goal.

"The Lord will grant you understanding in everything." Application also requires prayer. Apart from the Lord, our thinking will get us nowhere. We must handle the Bible prayerfully, asking the Author of Scripture to grant us understanding in everything. He must open our eyes to see clearly what he is saying. The psalmist realized this when he wrote, "Open my eyes that I may see wonderful things in your law" (Ps 119:18).

Application, therefore, begins on our knees. We must ask the Lord to reveal those areas of our lives that need to be transformed by his Word and his Spirit. We need the light of Scripture to shine in the dark recesses of our hearts. We need the Spirit of God to point out our areas of hardness and rebellion. We need the Great Physician to bind up the broken places in our lives and to heal our aching wounds.

Prayerful thought and thoughtful prayer—these are the vital components of meditation.

Case Studies in Meditation

Because meditation is so foreign to our fast-paced way of life, we can benefit from observing its impact in the lives of others. There are many case studies to choose from—in Scripture, in church history and in contemporary life.

Daniel is an outstanding biblical example of someone who combined thought and prayer in his study of Scripture. After many years of exile in Babylon, Daniel was astonished one day by what he read in the book of Jeremiah. As you read his account in Daniel 9, notice how many times he refers to words such as *understanding, insight* and *prayer:*

> In the first year of [Darius's] reign, I, Daniel, understood from the Scriptures, according to the word of the LORD given to Jeremiah the prophet, that the desolation of Jerusalem would last seventy years. So I turned to the Lord God and pleaded with him in prayer and petition, in fasting, and in sackcloth and ashes. . . . While I was speaking and praying, confessing my sin and the sin of my people Israel and making my request to the LORD my God for his holy hill—while I was still in prayer, Gabriel, the man I had seen in the earlier vision, came to me in swift flight about the time of the evening sacrifice. He instructed me and said to me, "Daniel, I have now come to give you insight and understanding. As soon as you began to pray, an answer was given, which I have come to tell you, for you are highly esteemed." (Dan 9:1-3, 20-23)

Because Daniel was a prophet, we often assume that his experience is completely different from our own. Admittedly, we cannot expect angelic visitations every time we open our Bibles and pray. However, Daniel was also human, a flesh-and-blood person as we are. He cared deeply about the people of Israel and the agony they had endured in Babylon. His compassion drove him to the same place it should drive us—to the Bible and to prayer. He longed to discover a link between God's eternal Word and the realities of everyday experience, and his longing was rewarded with insight from the Lord. The same is true today.

Church history also provides numerous examples of those whose meditation was rewarded with insight. One such person is John Woolman, an eighteenth-century Quaker whose study of Scripture led him to recognize the evils of slavery. Woolman did more than simply refuse to own slaves himself. As he continued to think and pray about slavery, the Holy Spirit convicted him about one area, then another and still another:

For the remainder of his life (he died in 1772) he spent about one month out of every year entreating others to free their slaves. . . . When he attended Quaker meetings, he quietly laid upon them the burden of his heart. If he stayed in a home where there were slaves, in the morning he would press some money in the hands of his host to give to a trusted slave with a view to purchasing freedom. He stopped wearing dyed suits because the dye for making men's suits was produced by slave labor. He refused to eat sugar, rum and molasses manufactured in the West Indies because they involved slave labor. . . . After 1763 he refused to ride on horseback or in conveyances because slaves could not do so.[3]

Such insights and applications did not come all at once. Meditation is an ongoing process in which life and Scripture continually interact, producing broader and deeper results. "In the matter of slavery and other areas John Woolman began to see that injustice comes about less from deliberate and planned effort than it does from *unthinking* and a *lack of sensitivity.*"[4]

One final "case study" is John Stott, the rector emeritus of All Souls Church in London. He provides a more recent example of someone who has taken time to meditate on God's Word. I have heard Stott speak many times, and I have always been impressed by his command of Scripture and contemporary life. Usually I am familiar with the passages he expounds. Yet as I listen to him, I begin to wonder whether I've ever really read the texts before. Where does his depth of understanding and wisdom come from? Stott writes:

> Speaking personally, I have always found it helpful to do as much of my sermon preparation as possible on my knees, with the Bible open before me, in prayerful study. This is not because I am a bibliolater and worship the Bible; but because I worship the God of the Bible and desire to humble myself before him and his revelation. Even while I am giving my mind to the study of the text, I pray earnestly that the eyes of my heart may be enlightened.[5]

A seminary professor once told my class that the only difference between us and the world's greatest Bible expositor was what we could see in the text before us. He might also have added *and in the world around us.* We may never be a Daniel or a John Woolman or a John Stott. Yet whoever we are, meditation can sharpen our spiritual eyesight so that, with God's help, we see and apply far more than we ever thought possible.

P A R T 2

SPECIFIC
TYPES OF
APPLICATION

CHAPTER SEVEN

APPLYING BIBLICAL COMMANDS

During the late sixties and early seventies, I was a student at the University of Texas. It was an exciting time to be on campus. Vietnam War protestors held huge rallies and marches. Long-haired hippies gathered for rock concerts and love-ins. With over forty thousand students on campus, something was always happening.

One day a group called the "Children of God" came to town. They pulled up in front of campus in a large bus covered with religious slogans, such as "Jesus Loves You" and "Drop Out for Jesus." Immediately they began passing out tracts, preaching judgment and salvation, and talking with anyone who would listen.

Our InterVarsity chapter didn't know quite what to make of them. Their zeal was contagious—and a bit frightening. They accused us of believing a watered-down version of Christianity. They claimed we were guilty of spiritual adultery, of embracing the harlot—Babylon the Great—because we had not dropped out of society.

To make matters worse, they supported their charges with Bible verses. They took us to passage after passage that seemed to support their position.

I remember one passage clearly—the story of the rich young man in Matthew 19. In that passage, a man came to Jesus and asked, "What good thing must I do to get eternal life?"

"If you want to enter life," Jesus answered, "obey the commandments."

"All these I have kept," the man replied. "What do I still lack?"

"If you want to be perfect," Jesus answered, "go, sell your possessions and give to the poor, and you will have treasure in heaven. Then come, follow me."

The Children of God had taken Jesus literally. They had sold or given away all that they had in order to follow Jesus. Why hadn't we? they demanded. Were we unwilling to obey Jesus' command?

For many of us, the whole encounter was very painful. Most of us were young Christians who tried to be sensitive to the Lord's leading. Although we couldn't refute their charges, we felt intuitively that they were wrong. But our common sense couldn't protect us completely from the fear that perhaps we were being disobedient to God.

In fact, a few days later we discovered that two very young Christians from our InterVarsity chapter had decided to join the

Children of God. Without a word to us, they drove off in the bus to the group's commune in south Texas. We never heard from them again.

Biblical commands are sometimes difficult to apply. Some people may say, "God said it. I believe it. And that settles it!" But it isn't always that simple. In this chapter I will try to provide some guidelines for applying the commands we find in Scripture.

Getting Motivated

Most of us don't like to be told what to do. We prefer to do what we want, when we want, with no interference from others. When someone orders us to do something, we inwardly rebel, even though outwardly we might obey.

My eighteen-month-old daughter is a good illustration of this tendency. She spends most of her time eagerly exploring our house and getting into everything. Frequently she plays with things that are forbidden to her—such as our stereo. It holds a natural fascination for her. The stereo has lights and motion, and Katie loves music. But it has a special allure because we have told her repeatedly, "No touch!" As soon as we first said that, our struggle became a contest of the wills. Even at her young age, she hates being told what to do!

Obviously, that kind of attitude—which is common to all of us—can become a major problem in our relationship with God. After all, he commands us to obey him in every area of our lives. How can we do so without feeling resentful or rebellious?

The New Testament gives us a clear answer to that question: "We love because he first loved us" (1 Jn 4:19). Our love is a *response* to God's love. Likewise, our obedience flows from our gratitude for what he has done for us.

This is true in both the Old and New Testaments. In the Old Testament, Israel's redemption from slavery in Egypt became the basis for the nation's obedience. At the beginning of the Ten Commandments, before the Lord had stated the first one, he reminded them: "I am the LORD your God, who brought you out of Egypt, out of the land of slavery" (Ex 20:2).

In the New Testament, our redemption from spiritual slavery becomes our primary motivation. John writes: "This is love: not that we loved God, but that he loved us and sent his Son as an atoning sacrifice for our sins" (1 Jn 4:10).

Because the biblical writers know this, they often go into great detail describing what God has done for us before asking us to do anything in response. Paul, for example, devotes three chapters in Ephesians to God's mercy and grace before giving us a single command. Likewise in Romans he spends eight chapters describing what God has done for us in Christ before urging us "in view of God's mercy, to offer your bodies as living sacrifices, holy and pleasing to God—which is your spiritual act of worship" (Rom 12:1).

Therefore, we must have a firm grasp and a deep appreciation of God's love before we can obey his commands with the proper motive. When our love for God begins to grow cold and our obedience falters, it is time to reread the accounts of Christ's love for us.

Applying Old Testament Commands

Old Testament commands usually give us the greatest difficulty. Rightly or wrongly, we assume that some Old Testament commands no longer apply to us. For example, in Deuteronomy

14:9-10 the Lord commands: "Of all the creatures living in the water, you may eat any that has fins and scales. But anything that does not have fins and scales you may not eat; for you it is unclean." I would have a terrible time obeying that command, since boiled shrimp is one of my favorite foods!

On the other hand, we feel sure that some Old Testament commands are still valid today, such as: "You shall not covet your neighbor's house. You shall not covet your neighbor's wife, or his manservant or maidservant, his ox or donkey, or anything that belongs to your neighbor" (Ex 20:17).

Yet for some reason we are less sure about a command that occurs only nine verses earlier: "Remember the Sabbath day by keeping it holy. Six days you shall labor and do all your work, but the seventh day is a Sabbath to the LORD your God. On it you shall not do any work" (Ex 20:8-10).

What's going on? Are we merely selecting those commands we want to obey and omitting the rest? What makes us think certain commands are still valid while others are not? In order to answer these questions, we need to understand some basic facts about the Old Testament.

First, we should be aware of the fact that the Old Testament contains over six hundred different commands. Most of these commands are found in the Pentateuch—that is, the first five books of the Old Testament: Genesis, Exodus, Leviticus, Numbers and Deuteronomy. The majority of them, in fact, are found in Exodus 20—Deuteronomy 26.

These five books, also known as the Law, contain various types of laws. Traditionally, these laws have been divided into three categories: moral laws, civil laws and ceremonial laws. However, a more recent scheme seems to be more helpful. It divides them into five categories: criminal laws, civil laws, family laws, cultic (ceremonial) laws and charitable laws.[1]

Second, we need to realize that the Old Testament is the record of God's covenant with Israel. In fact, the word *testament* means "covenant." A covenant was a binding agreement between two parties—in this case between the Lord and his people. The covenant not only contained detailed commands but also promises of blessing for obedience and curses for disobedience (see Deut 27—30).

Because Israel broke the old covenant, the Lord stated that one day he would establish a new covenant:

> "The time is coming," declares the LORD, "when I will make a new covenant with the house of Israel and with the house of Judah. . . . This is the covenant I will make with the house of Israel after that time," declares the LORD. "I will put my law in their minds and write it on their hearts. I will be their God, and they will be my people." (Jer 31:31, 33)

As Christians, we are no longer under the old covenant. Therefore, we are not subject to the requirements and conditions of that covenant. The author of Hebrews, after quoting the passage about the new covenant from Jeremiah 31, writes: "By calling this covenant 'new,' he has made the first one obsolete; and what is obsolete and aging will soon disappear" (Heb 8:13).

Does this mean the Old Testament has no application today? Of course not! It is still God's Word and was written for our benefit (2 Tim 3:16). But because we are no longer under the old covenant, we must use certain guidelines for applying Old Testament commands. For the sake of clarity, I will state these guidelines as questions that can be asked of any Old Testament command.

Is the command restated in the New Testament? Many Old Testament commands are also found in the New Testament. For example, most of the Ten Commandments are restated in one form or another.[2] Likewise, the two greatest commandments are repeated numerous times.[3] If a command has been restated within the new covenant, then it applies to us today.

Unfortunately, some have taken this guideline to an extreme. Robert McQuilkin writes:

> It is said that no teaching in the Old Testament is mandatory for the Christian unless it is repeated in the New Testament. However, to require a New Testament repetition is a dangerous mandate that is nowhere given in the New Testament. The New Testament authors and Jesus Himself treated the Old Testament (the only Bible they had) as the authoritative Word of God. It is not legitimate to set aside any Old Testament teaching without the authorization of subsequent revelation in the New Testament. Many Old Testament commands, such as those against bestiality and rape, are not repeated in the New Testament. Are they no longer normative?[4]

There are many other Old Testament laws which are not repeated in the New Testament. Clearly we need additional ways of determining whether such laws have any application today.

Is the command revoked in the New Testament? At times the New Testament explicitly sets aside an Old Testament command or institution. For example, the Old Testament contains numerous laws related to sacrifices, the temple and the priesthood. Yet according to the New Testament, these laws have been fulfilled by the once-for-all sacrifice of Christ (Heb 9—10).

The Old Testament also contains detailed dietary laws, forbidding the Israelites from eating such "unclean" items as pork or shellfish. Yet according to Mark's Gospel, Jesus revoked these laws. Mark writes: "In saying this, Jesus declared all foods 'clean' " (Mk 7:19; see also Acts 10).

Although these first two guidelines are important, they are rather limited in scope. They simply do not cover numerous Old Testament commands, which are neither repeated nor revoked in the New Testament. Some have suggested that the civil and ceremonial laws are no longer binding, and that only the moral laws are of value today. I find this suggestion unnecessarily restrictive and frustrating. After all, it relegates much of the Old Testament to oblivion. How then are we to regard those commands? A third guideline may clarify the matter.

What is the principle behind the Old Testament command? Although we are no longer under the Old Covenant, we need to remember that the laws of the Old Covenant reflect God's character. Likewise every law is an expression of one of the two greatest commandments regarding love for God and neighbor. This is true not only of the so-called moral laws but also of every other category of law. Therefore, the principles behind these laws should still be valid, even though some specific expressions of the laws may be obsolete.

For example, consider one of Israel's charitable laws, a command that was very specific to Israel's agricultural economy:

When you reap the harvest of your land, do not reap to the very edges of your field or gather the gleanings of your harvest. Do not go over your vineyard a second time or pick up the grapes that have fallen. Leave them for the poor and the alien. I am the LORD your God. (Lev 19:9-10)

In one sense, this command is no longer binding. It was written for farmers within ancient Israel. As such, it is not a legal requirement for us in the same way as it was for them—even for those today who own farms or vineyards.[5]

Yet this command clearly reveals God's practical concern for the poor and the alien. That concern is described numerous times in the Old Testament (Ex 22:21-27; 23:4-9; Lev 19:9-36; Deut 14:28-29; 15:12-14 and so on). The Lord wants us to care about such people because *he* cares about them. This passage illustrates that our care should be expressed in practical, tangible ways.

For example, some friends of mine decided that they should give their old clothes away rather than selling them at a garage sale. After all, their family had already gotten good use out of the clothes. For them, selling the clothes was equivalent to "going over [their] vineyard a second time." Although we may not feel bound to their specific application, we should seek to apply that passage in our own creative ways.

Next, consider one of Israel's criminal laws, one that has become infamous over the centuries. In two different places, the Lord commands that when someone has injured another, the court is to "show no pity: life for life, eye for eye, tooth for tooth, hand for hand, foot for foot" (Deut 19:21; see also 19:16-20; Ex 21:22-25).

To us the command seems gruesome and harsh—a law that is too barbaric to be part of our modern society. Yet we fail to realize that although the law was strict, it was also fair and curbed revenge. It demanded that the punishment fit the crime—a principle that is embodied in our own legal system. This principle stands in stark contrast to some societies in which theft, for example, is punishable by having one's hands cut off or by being executed. As it turns out, this infamous Old Testament law teaches us a valuable lesson we can apply today.

Finally, consider one of Israel's ceremonial laws, those which are often unceremoniously dismissed as no longer relevant. In Deuteronomy 26 the Lord gives a command about the firstfruits of the land. Although the passage is long, it is worth reading in its entirety:

When you have entered the land the LORD your God is giving you as an inheritance and have taken possession of it and settled in it, take some of the firstfruits of all that you produce from the soil of the land the LORD your God is giving you and put them in a basket. Then go to the place the LORD your God will choose as a dwelling for his Name. . . . The priest shall take the basket from your hands and set it down in front of the altar of the LORD your God. Then you shall declare before the LORD your God: "My father was a wandering Aramean, and he went down into Egypt with a few people and lived there and became a great nation, powerful and numerous. But the Egyptians mistreated us and made us suffer, putting us to hard labor. Then we cried out to the LORD . . . , and the LORD heard our voice and saw our misery, toil and oppression. So the LORD brought us out of Egypt with a mighty hand and an outstretched arm, with great terror and with miraculous signs and wonders. He brought us to this place and gave us this land, a land flowing with milk and honey; and now I bring the firstfruits of the soil that you, O LORD, have given me." Place the basket before the LORD your God and bow down before him. And you and the Levites and the aliens among you shall rejoice in all the good things the LORD your God has given to you and your household. (vv. 1-2, 4-11)

Although the tabernacle and temple are no longer standing, and we are not residents of the Promised Land, the principle behind this command is clear: We owe everything to the Lord. He is the One who hears and answers our prayers, who delivers us from evil, who gives us a place to live, who provides us with food to eat and clothes to wear. As James puts it: "Every good and perfect gift is from above, coming down from the Father" (Jas 1:17).

We should acknowledge God's goodness to us both privately and publicly, rejoicing and giving thanks for what he has done in our lives. As an expression of our appreciation, we should give back to him a portion of what he has given us. One church in our community has a "First Fruits Festival" every year in which people give their "first fruits" to the Lord in an evening service. One person gave the first check he earned in his new business. Another gave the church library a copy of a book he had just had published. A woman who had been supported by the church during a personal crisis decided to give time each week to others in crisis situations. Such examples only begin to scratch the surface. Obviously, the principle behind this "outdated" command has powerful implications for us today.

Applying New Testament Commands

Applying most New Testament commands is simply a matter of following the guidelines discussed in previous chapters. First, we need to understand the original situation. Then we need to determine whether our situation is identical or comparable to it. If it is identical, then the command can be applied directly. If it is not identical, then we must seek to discover the principle behind the command and apply it to comparable situations that we do come up against today.

For example, consider the passage about the rich young man, the one used by the Children of God. This passage is a bit more difficult than most, but the guidelines above can help us unravel its meaning.

For the sake of clarity, I'll quote the passage again in full:

Now a man came up to Jesus and asked, "Teacher, what good thing must I do to get eternal life?"

"Why do you ask me about what is good?" Jesus replied. "There is only One who is good. If you want to enter life, obey the commandments."

"Which ones?" the man inquired.

Jesus replied, " 'Do not murder, do not commit adultery, do not steal, do not give false testimony, honor your father and mother,' and 'love your neighbor as yourself.' "

"All these things I have kept," the young man said. "What do I still lack?"

Jesus answered, "If you want to be perfect, go, sell your possessions and give to the poor, and you will have treasure in heaven. Then come, follow me."

When the young man heard this, he went away sad, because he had great wealth. (Mt 19:16-22)

The first thing we should notice is the young man's question: "What good thing must I do to get eternal life?" His question can be taken in one of two ways. It may simply be a legitimate question about salvation, similar to the Philippian jailer's question: "What must I do to be saved?" (Acts 16:30). However, it is also possible to put the emphasis on the word *do*—"What must I *do* to be saved?"—inferring that the young man thought he could do something to merit eternal life.

Notice, too, Jesus' response: "If you want to enter life, obey the commandments." If we were teaching a course on Evangelism 101, and a student gave this answer, we would fail him on the spot! From the moment we first become Christians, we are taught that no one can be saved by keeping the commandments; salvation comes only by faith.

Jesus' response, therefore, should immediately arouse our curiosity. Why did he give that answer to the man? Why does he point him to the Law rather than to faith?

We should also note the particular commandments Jesus mentioned. Five of them are from the Ten Commandments. You may recall that the first four commandments describe our relationship with God and the other six our relationship with our neighbor. For some reason, Jesus omits the first four and the last commandment, the one about covetousness.

The other commandment Jesus quotes is one of the two great commandments. Just as he omitted the four commandments about our relationship with God, so here Jesus omits the greatest commandment—the one about loving God with all our heart, soul and strength (Deut 6:5).

Again, our curiosity should be aroused. Why did Jesus only mention the commandments related to neighbors and omit any reference to the man's relationship with God?

Obviously, the young man felt very confident about his relationship to his neighbor. " 'All these I have kept,' the young man said" (Mt 19:20).

If we had been Jesus, I can imagine how we would have responded to such a cocky assertion: "You may have kept them outwardly," we might say, "but you haven't kept them inwardly—where it counts! Have you ever hated someone or lusted after a woman in your heart?" And so on.

Jesus takes a different approach. "If you want to be perfect, go, sell your possessions and give to the poor, and you will have treasure in heaven. Then come, follow me" (v. 21). After hearing this, the man went away sad, because he "had great wealth" (v. 22).

If we put all the pieces back together, we can see the original situation much more clearly. The young man had the kind of self-confident attitude that sometimes characterizes the rich. He thought he could do something to earn eternal life, perhaps in the same way that he had earned his wealth. When confronted with commandments about his neighbor, he in essence replied: "No problem!"

Jesus knew, however, that the man had not kept all the commandments. When he asked the young man to sell his possessions, Jesus exposed the man's true spiritual condition. The man cared more about his wealth than about God. Although he claimed to have kept the commandments, he had broken the most important one—the commandment about loving God above all else. Because he had made wealth his god, he had also broken the first, second and tenth commandments against idolatry and covetousness. Since he was unwilling to renounce his idol, he could not follow Jesus.

Now that we have understood the original situation, we are in a position to ask what principle is being taught in this passage. It is not necessarily a command to sell our possessions, for we can have other idols, such as power, sex or fame. What Jesus demands is that we put him first. If we have made power our god, then we must be willing to give up that power. If we worship sex or fame, we must be willing to renounce them as well.

Nothing must be allowed to usurp Jesus' rightful place as Lord of our lives.[6]

What the Children of God had failed to realize is that possessions are not the key element in this passage, but rather a variable. The key element—or in this case the key question to ask—is "Who or what has the supreme place in our lives?"

By first understanding the original situation, and then finding the principle behind that situation, you will be able to apply most New Testament commands. However, there are certain exceptions.

As I have mentioned previously, most books of the Bible were written for a specific purpose to a specific audience, facing specific problems. Therefore, in order to apply the message of these books, we often need to move up a level in the pyramid by finding a general principle that is applicable today.

Yet it is also true that many New Testament commands have the opposite problem. Consider, for example, a well-known passage in Colossians:

> Therefore, as God's chosen people, holy and dearly loved, clothe yourselves with compassion, kindness, humility, gentleness and patience. Bear with each other and forgive whatever grievances you may have against one another. Forgive as the Lord forgave you. And over all these virtues put on love, which binds them all together in perfect unity. (3:12-14)

With passages like this, we don't need to find general principles behind the specific situations. Rather, we need to find specific situations to go with the general principles! Paul's commands are so general, so high up on the pyramid, that we need to move down a level or two in order to apply them to the everyday situations we face. In other words, the general nature of the commands allows them to apply to an almost limitless variety of situations. There are hundreds of ways we can express compassion, kindness, humility, gentleness, patience and love to those around us. Likewise, there are numerous situations in which we need to forgive others as Christ has forgiven us. However, because Paul does not identify what those situations are, we must think creatively about ways in which they might apply today.

How, for example, could my wife and I express love to those in our church? We could open our home to lonely people. We could help the elderly with projects around their homes. We could become involved in hospital visitation or take meals to those who are sick. We could volunteer for those jobs no one else wants, such as nursery duty or cleanup after socials. We could become a listening ear to those who are hurting.

The list is endless. But we haven't really applied Paul's commands—or any other commands in Scripture—until we begin thinking about such a list, asking God for wisdom and guidance, and then acting on it.

APPLYING
BIBLICAL
EXAMPLES

Awoman I once knew wanted to know whether the man she was dating was the one she should marry. She told the Lord that if her boyfriend would send her a dozen yellow roses, she would know he was the one for her. I'm sure she saw points of similarity between her situation and that of Gideon. But not having a fleece available, she decided to use roses. (They're more romantic than a wet fleece anyway!) Surprisingly, the man did send her yellow roses and asked her to marry him. She accepted.

Now, I would not presume to say that my friend was wrong in marrying this man. I'm even willing to admit that God may have used the roses to confirm her decision to marry him. After all, God is gracious and often works in spite of us. But was that a proper application of Scripture?

A more celebrated example is the early Mormon practice of polygamy. Obviously, the Mormons saw a parallel between their situation and that of many of the biblical characters. Abraham, Jacob, David and Solomon (to name only a few) all had more than one wife. In fact, Solomon had seven hundred wives and three hundred concubines (1 Kings 11:3). Compared to Solomon, the Mormons were models of self-restraint! But were they correctly applying Scripture or were they misapplying it?

These two incidents illustrate some of the thorny problems we encounter when applying biblical examples. How can we know whether an example recorded in Scripture applies to our situation? How can we determine whether the example is merely a record of what happened or a divinely intended pattern for us to follow? This chapter will seek to answer these and other related questions.

The Nature of Biblical Examples

Since over forty per cent of the Bible is historical narrative, the Scriptures are full of biblical examples. In the Old Testament we meet such characters as Abraham, Joseph, Moses, Joshua, Deborah, Saul, David and Esther. In the New Testament we are introduced to Elizabeth, John the Baptist, Mary and Martha, Peter, James, Paul, Barnabas and a host of others.

We can learn valuable lessons—both positive and negative—from the lives of these people. The author of Hebrews runs out of space in describing the outstanding exploits of biblical heroes:

And what more shall I say? I do not have time to tell about Gideon, Barak, Samson, Jephthah, David, Samuel and the prophets, who through faith conquered kingdoms, adminis-

tered justice, and gained what was promised; who shut the
mouths of lions, quenched the fury of the flames, and escaped
the edge of the sword; whose weakness was turned to
strength; and who became powerful in battle and routed foreign armies. Women received back their dead, raised to life
again. Others were tortured and refused to be released, so that
they might gain a better resurrection. Some faced jeers and
flogging, while still others were chained and put in prison.
They were stoned; they were sawed in two; they were put to
death by the sword. They went about in sheepskins and goat-
skins, destitute, persecuted and mistreated—the world was
not worthy of them. (11:32-38)

Clearly there are many excellent examples in the Bible. The difficulty, however, is knowing which examples we are to follow
and which we should avoid.

Frequently, the biblical authors tell us *explicitly* whether a person or group of people is a good or a bad example. For instance,
during the exodus and wilderness wanderings, Israel's actions
are often evaluated by Moses or the Lord himself.

Likewise, in the books of 1 and 2 Kings, the author leaves
little doubt about how we should view the actions of the various
kings. In most cases the account begins by stating who became
king, when he came to power, how long he reigned and whether
he did or did not do what is right in the eyes of the Lord.

Many biblical examples, however, do not include an explicit
statement about whether the actions are right or wrong. Sometimes this is because the author gives *implicit* approval or disap-
proval of what is done.

For instance, when Rahab the prostitute lies to protect the two
spies sent to look over Jericho, the author does not say: "Rahab

did right in the eyes of the Lord." Nor is there any implicit approval of her lying, either in the book of Joshua or elsewhere in Scripture.

However, the author is careful to record Rahab's statement of faith in the Lord, which formed the basis for her actions: "I know that the LORD has given this land to you and that a great fear of you has fallen on us, so that all who live in this country are melting in fear because of you" (Josh 2:9). The New Testament confirms what is implicit in the narrative: "By faith the prostitute Rahab, because she welcomed the spies, was not killed with those who were disobedient" (Heb 11:31).

The most difficult biblical examples to apply are those which contain neither an explicit nor implicit evaluation of a person's actions. For example, was it wrong for Abram to take Hagar as his wife when Sarai was barren (Gen 16)? We may have our own opinion about the matter, but the author simply does not tell us. Were the apostles right in casting lots to determine who should take the place of Judas (Acts 1:12-26)? Many people have claimed that their method was wrong and that the Lord later overrode their decision by appointing Paul as the twelfth apostle (Acts 9). However, they are reading into the account something which Luke remains silent about.

The method we use for applying a biblical example will depend on whether it is an explicit example, an implicit example or one which is merely recorded without comment. Let's begin by looking more closely at explicit examples.

Applying Explicit Examples

When studying biblical examples, the first item to note is whether the author comments on the nature of the example. Does the author or the Lord himself say that the example is good or bad? And is there a specific reference that says the person did something right or wrong?

For example, our Bible-study group recently began a series on little-known characters of the Bible. Instead of looking at the lives of the more popular biblical heroes—Abraham, Moses, David and so on—we focused on some of the more obscure figures, people like Hannah, Micaiah, Jonah, Naaman the leper and Jehoshaphat.

One of the characters we studied was Josiah (2 Kings 22—23). Josiah became king during a dark period of Judah's history. Both his father, Amon, and the previous king, Manasseh, had done evil in the eyes of the Lord. In fact, Manasseh is blamed for the Babylonian invasion (2 Kings 24:1-4), although his sins were merely the culmination of years of apostasy and unbelief.

Josiah was only eight years old when he came to the throne, but he reigned for thirty-one years. At the beginning of the account of Josiah's reign, the author states explicitly that he "did what was right in the eyes of the LORD and walked in all the ways of his father David, not turning aside to the right or to the left" (22:2).

The author also tells us what Josiah did right. He began by appointing men to repair the temple, which had deteriorated during the reigns of his predecessors. But his life took a dramatic turn while work on the temple was underway. During the repairs, Hilkiah the priest made a remarkable discovery. He reported: "I have found the Book of the Law in the temple of the LORD" (22:8).

Biblical scholars believe the "Book of the Law" was either a copy of the Pentateuch or else the book of Deuteronomy. Evidently, the spiritual life of the nation had sunk so low that they had even misplaced and forgotten about the Scriptures.

When Josiah heard the words of the Book of the Law, he tore his robes (a sign of mourning and repentance) and began a remarkable series of reforms. First, he gathered together all the leaders in Judah and all the people in Jerusalem and read to them the entire Book of the Law. Then the king "renewed the covenant in the presence of the LORD—to follow the LORD and keep his commands, regulations and decrees with all his heart and all his soul, thus confirming the words of the covenant written in this book" (23:3).

Next, he purged Jerusalem of every evidence of idolatry. He removed from the temple the articles made for Baal. He did away with the pagan priests appointed by the previous kings of Judah. He desecrated the high places used for sacrifices and burning incense. And he pulled down the altars to the pagan gods and smashed them to pieces. Finally, when the region had been purified of idolatry, Josiah ordered the people to celebrate the Passover, "as it is written in this Book of the Covenant" (v. 21). Throughout the passage, the author describes in explicit detail why Josiah is a good example to follow.

Of course, the fact that Josiah is a good example does not remove the necessity of asking, A good example of what? Are we to tear our clothes, demolish local pagan temples, execute cult leaders and then offer animal sacrifices? Certainly not. Just as in other passages of Scripture, we need to look for the general principle behind this account.

What is that principle? After the author of 2 Kings concludes his description of Josiah's reign, he gives this remarkable eulogy: "Neither before nor after Josiah was there a king like him who turned to the LORD as he did—with all his heart and with all his soul and with all his strength, in accordance with all the Law of Moses" (23:25).

Josiah illustrates what it means to keep the greatest commandment. He loved the Lord "with all his heart and with all his soul and with all his strength." How did he love him? By reading and obeying the Law of Moses—the appropriate response for a king under the Old Covenant. Today we too are called to turn to the Lord with all our heart, soul and strength. But we do so in ways appropriate to the New Covenant.

Dwight L. Moody is one person in recent times who chose to follow Josiah's example. During Moody's first preaching tour in England, a close friend of his remarked: "The world has yet to see what God can do through a man who is totally committed to him." At that strategic point in his career, Moody decided: "I will be that man." From that day on, his life and ministry were never the same.

Applying Implicit Examples

Frequently, the biblical authors aren't so explicit about whether an example is good or bad. We are left with uncertainty about what lessons we are to learn from the characters we read about. Yet if we study the accounts carefully, we will often find that their message is implicit in the details of the narrative.

For example, consider the story of Jonah. The Lord commanded Jonah to "go to the great city of Nineveh and preach against it, because its wickedness has come up before me" (1:1-2). Yet instead of obeying the word of the Lord, Jonah decided to run away. He headed for the seaport town of Joppa and boarded a ship bound for Tarshish, a place traditionally identified with Spain. If you consult a map of the Mediterranean region, you will discover that Tarshish was over two thousand miles in the opposite direction from Nineveh. When Jonah decided to run, he didn't fool around!

At this point, the story is familiar to most of us. While Jonah was on board the ship, the Lord caused a violent storm to arise which threatened to sink the ship. After the sailors discovered that the storm was a result of Jonah's disobedience, they threw him overboard, as Jonah himself requested.

As Jonah was sinking beneath the waves, the Lord provided a great fish to swallow him, and he remained in its belly for three days and nights. But after Jonah cried out to the Lord for deliverance, the fish vomited Jonah onto dry land (2:10).

I laugh every time I read the next two verses: "Then the word of the LORD came to Jonah a second time: 'Go to the great city of Nineveh and proclaim to it the message I give you' (3:1-2). What a classic example of biblical understatement! Having subjected Jonah to a terrifying storm, the indignity of being thrown overboard, the danger of drowning, and the watery grave of the fish's stomach, the Lord says in essence: "Now will you obey me?" Jonah may have been rebellious, but he wasn't stupid. Verse 3 states that "Jonah obeyed the word of the LORD and went to Nineveh."

Surprisingly, the people of Nineveh, from the king all the way down to the livestock, repented at the preaching of Jonah. But instead of being thrilled at his evangelistic triumph, Jonah was appalled. He sat down outside the city, hoping that fire from heaven would still come and destroy the people of Nineveh.

The last words we hear from Jonah are not an expression of compassion but of anger. He tells the Lord he would like to die because a vine that had shaded him from the sun had withered. The Lord responds by saying:

You have been concerned about this vine, though you did not tend it or make it grow. It sprang up overnight and died overnight. But Nineveh has more than a hundred and twenty thousand people who cannot tell their right hand from their left, and many cattle as well. Should I not be concerned about that great city?" (4:10-11)

What is the lesson we are to learn from this brief, humorous and somewhat pathetic story? The author doesn't tell us directly. Of course, we might conclude from the last two verses of the book that we are to have compassion for the lost—but there is more to it than that. The full message doesn't surface until we look more closely at the details of the narrative.

The most important detail to notice is the city of Nineveh itself, which is so prominent in the story. Why was Jonah so reluctant to go there? Was he merely afraid, as some have suggested, or was there some other reason? And why was he disappointed when the Lord spared the city rather than being overjoyed at God's grace and the large number of conversions? The answers to these questions would have been familiar to the original readers of the book, but they only become clear to us if we do a little historical and cultural research into Nineveh and its relationship with Israel.

By consulting a Bible dictionary or encyclopedia, we discover that Nineveh was the capital of Assyria, the most powerful nation on earth and an enemy of Israel. In fact, Assyria later conquered Israel in 722 B.C.

Against this backdrop, Jonah's actions are easier to understand. His motive for running away was not primarily fear but hatred of his enemies. Likewise, his anger at Nineveh's repentance was ethnically motivated. He didn't want those filthy, no-good pagans to be saved. Let them burn!

In essence, then, the book of Jonah is a plea for the people of Israel to have compassion on all people—even those they consider their enemies:

> In this story of God's loving concern for all people, Nineveh, the great menace to Israel, is representative of the Gentiles. Correspondingly, stubbornly reluctant Jonah represents Israel's jealousy of her favored relationship with God and her unwillingness to share the Lord's compassion with the nations.
>
> The book depicts the larger scope of God's purpose for Israel: that she might rediscover the truth of his concern for the whole creation and that she might better understand her own role in carrying out that concern.[1]

Clearly, Jonah is meant to be a negative rather than a positive example. He embodies the narrow-mindedness and racial prejudice that has plagued God's people throughout the centuries. In subtle but powerful ways, the author points out what is wrong with Jonah's attitude—and possibly ours as well—and urges us to show to others the kind of compassion God has shown to us.

As we try to evaluate the lives of the people recorded in Scripture, it is crucial to look for evidence within the text. Sometimes this evidence can be uncovered by researching the historical and cultural background of the passage—as in the case of Jonah. At other times the key may be the literary context. By carefully reading the chapters that come before and after the story, we can discern how the passage functions as a part of the larger narrative. Or we may need to look for a recurring theme in the passage or book. Our goal throughout this process is to discover the message implicit in the story. The biblical authors aren't attempting to hide that message from us. But like all good writers, they know we will have greater appreciation for something we work for and discover on our own.

Applying Other Types of Examples

What do we do when an author doesn't tell us the purpose of an example or comment—either explicitly or implicitly—on whether it is a good or bad example? If this type of situation occurred rarely in Scripture, perhaps we wouldn't need to be concerned. Unfortunately, it is fairly common.

In such cases we need to rely on truths or principles taught elsewhere in Scripture. The biblical authors expect us to have at least a basic knowledge of God's Word. In the Old Testament, it is assumed that the reader is familiar with the Law. In the New Testament, we are expected to know something about Christian theology and ethics. These assumptions on the part of biblical writers often explain why they don't comment on a person's actions. They expect us to know enough to draw our own conclusions!

This type of biblical example falls into two categories. Some examples are endorsed by later biblical authors who wish to illustrate a principle they are teaching. Once we know what that principle is, we can understand it more clearly by reading about the example in its original setting.

Other examples lack this biblical endorsement. The original author did not intend them to function as examples, and they are not used in that way by other biblical authors. Still, they may be excellent illustrations of biblical principles taught elsewhere. But it is up to us to make the connection between the examples and the principles they illustrate.

Let's look at examples that fall into each category.

Biblically endorsed example: Philemon and Onesimus. Have you ever wondered why the book of Philemon is in the Bible? It is only twenty-five verses long, contains no profound theology and is generally ignored by the Christian public.

A few years ago I was so intrigued by this question that I decided to teach a Sunday-school class on Philemon—to force myself to find something of value in this measly epistle.

What I discovered surprised me. I hadn't gotten any answers from Philemon because I was asking the wrong questions. It contains almost no direct teaching. Instead, it is a practical example of truths taught elsewhere in Scripture. Philemon illustrates how we can mend fractured relationships.

In order to understand this brief letter, we must know something about the situation which caused it to be written. Philemon was a native of Colossae, a town in Asia Minor. He and his wife, Apphia, and their son, Archippus, were hosts for a church which met in their home (vv. 1-2).

Evidently, one of Philemon's slaves, a man named Onesimus, ran away and perhaps stole something for his journey (v. 18)—an offense punishable by death under Roman law. He kept on running until he had reached Rome, a city over a thousand miles away. There he met the apostle Paul and was converted under his ministry (v. 10). Now Paul was sending him back to Colossae to be reconciled to Philemon (v. 12).

It is significant to note that Philemon was written the same time as the letter to the Colossians. Both letters were delivered by a man named Tychicus and by Onesimus (Col 4:7-9). Because Colossians contains so much direct teaching about Christ and Christian relationships, Paul evidently felt no need to repeat that teaching in his note to Philemon. Instead, he assumed that teaching and allowed it to be a backdrop for his appeal for reconciliation.

For example, after his opening thanksgiving and prayer for Philemon, Paul writes: "Therefore, although in Christ I could be bold and order you to do what you ought to do, yet I appeal to you on the basis of love" (vv. 8-9). What was it that Paul thought Philemon ought to do? Clearly he thought he should be reconciled to Onesimus. Yet he never tells Philemon—or us, for that matter—why that was his obligation, because he had already given the following instructions in Colossians:

Here there is no Greek or Jew, circumcised or uncircumcised, barbarian, Scythian, slave or free, but Christ is all, and is in all.

Therefore, as God's chosen people, holy and dearly loved, clothe yourselves with compassion, kindness, humility, gentleness and patience. Bear with each other and forgive whatever grievances you may have against one another. Forgive as the Lord forgave you. And over all these virtues put on love, which binds them all together in perfect unity.

Let the peace of Christ rule in your hearts, since as members of one body you were called to peace. (Col 3:11-15)

How does Paul's letter to Philemon reinforce these verses in Colossians? It illustrates three principles of reconciliation:

1: Reconciliation requires love. Paul appeals to Philemon on the basis of love (v. 9). This is the ultimate motive for mending any fractured relationship. It is also the foundation for maintaining our relationships in Christ (Col 3:14).

2: Reconciliation is required. Paul reminds Philemon that he could order him to do what he ought to do (v. 8). Even if we can't bring ourselves to love a person, we are still required to forgive them and be reconciled to them, because Christ has forgiven us (Col 3:13).

3: Reconciliation is a family matter. Paul tells Philemon: "Perhaps the reason he was separated from you for a little while was that you might have him back for good—no longer as a slave, but better than a slave, as a dear brother" (vv. 15-16). The fact that we are members of one family in Christ provides a powerful incentive for reconciliation (Col 3:11, 15).

The book of Philemon is clearly a biblically endorsed example of principles taught elsewhere in Scripture. Paul intended the letter to be read in conjunction with Colossians, so that the latter could provide the theological and ethical framework for his words to Philemon.

This fact is supported by another brief section of Colossians. Scholars have noted that in the nine verses that Paul devotes to rules for Christian households (Col 3:18—4:1), only four verses cover relationships between wives and husbands, children and parents, and fathers and children; but Paul spends five verses discussing the relationship between slaves and masters. It seems highly unlikely that this is mere coincidence. Obviously, Paul wants to emphasize the kind of relationship that should exist between Philemon and Onesimus.

Paul's letter to Philemon is only one of many biblically endorsed examples found in Scripture. Paul uses Abraham's faith in God's promise of Isaac as an illustration of justification by faith (Rom 4:18-25). James uses Elijah as an example of effective prayer (Jas 5:13-18). Peter uses Sarah as an example of submissiveness (1 Pet 3:1-6).

When other biblical authors suggest that we follow a certain example, we can do so even though that application was not endorsed by the original author. But what should we do when a biblical example lacks the endorsement of both the original author and the later authors of Scripture?

Unendorsed example: Joseph and Potiphar's wife. As we read about certain biblical characters, we will search in vain for explicit statements about what they have done right or wrong or even implicit clues about the lessons we are to learn. We may also find that no other biblical authors give us any help in applying those examples. Still, the story may bring to mind principles we have learned in Scripture and bring those principles to life in new and revealing ways. One incident in Joseph's life is that kind of example.

The Joseph narrative covers Genesis 37—50. The story shows how God preserved the nation of Israel during a time of famine by bringing Joseph into a position of power in Egypt. All of the major sections of the narrative function within this framework.

One section of the narrative describes Joseph's temptation by Potiphar's wife (Gen 39). The author tells us that Potiphar bought Joseph from the Ishmaelites who had taken him to Egypt. Because the Lord was with Joseph and caused him to be successful, Potiphar put him in charge of his household.

At this point the plot thickens. Potiphar's wife noticed that Joseph was "well-built and handsome" and said, "Come to bed with me!" (v. 7). Although Joseph refused, Potiphar's wife didn't give up. Day after day she begged Joseph to sleep with her, even though he rejected her advances.

Then one day Joseph went into the house to attend to his duties and noticed that none of the household servants were inside. Although the author doesn't tell us, it may be that Potiphar's wife had deliberately sent them away.

When she saw Joseph, she tried to force the situation. She grabbed Joseph's cloak and said again: "Come to bed with me!" This time she wasn't going to let him get away! Yet the author tells us that Joseph "left his cloak in her hand and ran out of the house" (v. 12).

Within the larger framework of the narrative, this incident tells us how Joseph ended up in prison and eventually was brought before Pharaoh. It is doubtful that the author intended Joseph to be an example of how to resist temptation. If that were his intention, there is no way to prove it.

Yet common sense tells us that Joseph is an excellent illustration of a biblical truth taught elsewhere. His actions are a vivid example of Paul's commands, "Flee from sexual immorality" and "Flee the evil desires of youth" (1 Cor 6:18; 2 Tim 2:22). Joseph followed these commands literally, and there are many occasions when we would be wise to do the same.

Although this type of example can be very illuminating, it also has its dangers. Because it is not a divinely intended example, it may or may not be a good illustration of a biblical truth taught elsewhere. And even if it is a good illustration, it is merely an illustration of that truth and does not carry the same weight as the truth itself.

With this type of example we also face the danger of trying to make the details of the story teach more than the principle itself. We need to keep in mind that the story is not the source of the principle but is only an illustration of it.

Another Look at Gideon

Before concluding this chapter, it might be worthwhile to look again at Gideon's fleece and how his example was used by my friend.

The story of Gideon and the fleece occurs in Judges 6. During that period, the people of Israel had done evil in the eyes of the Lord, and so he had allowed the Midianites to oppress them for seven years. When the Israelites finally cried out to the Lord for help, he appointed Gideon as their deliverer.

The angel of the Lord appeared to Gideon and said, "Go in the strength you have and save Israel out of Midian's hand. Am I not sending you?" (v. 14).

When Gideon asked how someone as lowly as he could possibly deliver Israel, the Lord assured him: "I will be with you, and you will strike down all the Midianites together" (v. 16).

Gideon still wasn't satisfied. He replied, "If now I have found favor in your eyes, give me a sign that it is really you talking to me" (v. 17).

Then Gideon ran and prepared a meal for the angel of the Lord. When he returned with the meal, Gideon was told to "take the meat and the unleavened bread, place them on this rock, and pour out the broth" (v. 20). And Gideon did so. "With the tip of the staff that was in his hand, the angel of the LORD touched the meat and the unleavened bread. Fire flared from the rock, consuming the meat and the bread. And the angel of the LORD disappeared" (v. 21).

Having witnessed this miracle, did Gideon go out and fight the Midianites? Unfortunately not. He still refused to believe the Lord's repeated promises and assurances. This is where the infamous fleece comes in.

Gideon said to God, "If you will save Israel by my hand as you have promised—look, I will place a wool fleece on the threshing floor. If there is dew only on the fleece and all the ground is dry, then I will know that you will save Israel by my hand, as you said." And that is what happened. Gideon rose early the next day; he squeezed the fleece and wrung out the dew—a bowlful of water. (vv. 36-38)

Now that the Lord had given him this extra assurance, did Gideon finally go out and fight the Midianites? Well, not exactly. The text continues:

Then Gideon said to God, "Do not be angry with me. Let me make just one more request. Allow me one more test with the fleece. This time make the fleece dry and the ground covered with dew." That night God did so. Only the fleece was dry; all the ground was covered with dew. (vv. 39-40)

Before commenting on my friend's use of this text, it might be worthwhile to ask what kind of example this is. Obviously, it is not an explicit example of how to discern God's will, for the author never says, "This is the way it should be done."

Could Gideon be an implicit example of how we should obtain guidance? Once again, there is nothing in the text to suggest that his actions should be a model for our own. If anything, the story implies just the opposite. In this situation Gideon seems to be a classic example of unbelief.

Might Gideon's use of the fleece be an example of a biblical truth taught elsewhere? Certainly there are many passages in the Bible that assure us of God's guidance. But we are never told to put a "fleece" before the Lord in order to determine the truth of his promises. Instead we are to rest on the promises themselves, believing that God will be faithful to what he has said.

Now for my friend. All that I have mentioned previously indicates that she should never have followed Gideon's example of unbelief. Yet having decided to do so, she didn't really follow his example.

Notice that God had not given her a promise that her boyfriend would marry her. Yet the Lord had given Gideon a promise of victory before he put out the fleece. Notice too that her "fleece" of roses didn't demand anything miraculous from the Lord. Her boyfriend's response might have merely been coincidence. The Lord's response to Gideon defied the laws of nature. Finally, it should be pointed out that she did not ask for yellow roses one day and red roses the next. If she wanted to follow Gideon's example, why not go the whole way?

Having said all this, I want to reiterate that God is gracious and often accommodates himself to our weakness. Clearly this was the case with Gideon and with my friend. Yet this gives us no justification for using biblical examples in ways they were never intended. There are enough good examples to keep us busy for a lifetime!

CHAPTER NINE

APPLYING
BIBLICAL
PROMISES

*T*he world will end in 1843!" *William Miller came to that star-*
tling conclusion after two years of intense study, particularly in
the book of Daniel. "I was thus brought, in 1818, at the close
of my two-year study of the Scriptures, to the solemn conclusion, that in about twenty-five years from that time all the affairs
of our present state would be wound up."[1]

After four more years of study confirmed his previous conclusions, Miller declared his views publicly in 1831. Christ would
return sometime between March 21, 1843, and March 21, 1844.

The response, in some circles, was enthusiastic. In 1834
Miller had so many speaking engagements that he decided to
become a full-time Baptist minister. For the next several years,

he proclaimed his message to an ever-growing group of followers.

When the eagerly awaited year arrived, however, the Lord did
not return as predicted. This was a terrible blow to both Miller
and his followers. But before their disappointment had become
too intense, one of Miller's disciples found an error in his calculations. Christ would actually return, he announced, on Oc-
tober 22, 1844![2]

With renewed enthusiasm, groups of Millerites excitedly
gathered in homes and meeting places on the morning of the
twenty-second. Throughout the day they waited joyously, expecting the Lord to come any moment. Sometime after midnight,
their disappointment became overwhelming. Disillusioned and
dejected, they gave up their hopes and returned to their homes.

Over a hundred years later, in 1973, a tragedy of a different
sort occurred. A couple in Indiana became convinced that physical healing was promised unconditionally to anyone who would
claim it. When their seven-month-old daughter became seriously
ill because of a congenital liver defect, they ignored the advice
of doctors. Instead, they called their pastor, who recommended
prayer. The couple prayed for their child from about noon on
Christmas eve until about 4:00 P.M. on Christmas day. At that
time they stopped praying because their baby had died.[3]

The apostle Peter tells us that God "has given us his very great
and precious promises, so that through them you may partici-
pate in the divine nature and escape the corruption in the world"
(2 Pet 1:4). These promises have given hope and strong encouragement to Christians throughout the centuries. Unfortunately,
they can also be abused—with tragic consequences.

How can we know when a biblical promise applies to us? How

can we be sure we are exercising genuine faith rather than foolish optimism? This chapter will offer guidelines for applying the
promises we find in God's Word.

Before applying a biblical promise, we must ask a few questions about the nature of the promise. These questions can help
us determine whether the promise is meant for us.

Is the Promise Part of the Old or New Covenant?

Like biblical commands, the promises of Scripture are part of
either the Old or New Covenants. Because we are no longer
under the Old Covenant, we cannot assume that the promises
of that covenant *directly* apply to us. In fact, most of them do not.
Such promises are usually associated with the blessings God
promised the people of Israel if they obeyed his Law (Lev 26;
Deut 28).

For example, Malachi 3:10 is often quoted today as an incentive for tithing. One author writes:

The exhortation of Malachi concerning tithing contains with
it a promise of blessing. "Bring the full tithes into the storehouse, that there may be food in my house; and thereby put
me to the test, says the LORD of hosts, if I will not open the
windows of heaven for you and pour down for you an over-
flowing blessing" (Mal 3:10). This is a promise which evan-
gelicals will not want to overlook given the foreboding expectations of the 1980s.[4]

I am not suggesting that tithing is inappropriate today. Nor do
I mean to imply that there are no comparable New Testament
promises, such as those in 2 Corinthians 9. Yet there are several
reasons why we should not view this promise as directly applicable to us today.

First, Malachi's promise is clearly linked to the promises of the Old Covenant in Deuteronomy 28. Moses writes:

If you fully obey the LORD your God and carefully follow all his commands I give you today, . . . the LORD will open the heavens, the storehouse of his bounty, to send rain on your land in season and to bless all the work of your hands. You will lend to many nations but will borrow from none." (vv. 1, 12)

Even the wording of Malachi's promise is reminiscent of the blessing promised under the Old Covenant. This is not surprising, since the prophets were divinely ordained enforcers of that covenant.[5] Fee and Stuart write:

The prophets were inspired by God to present the essential content of the covenant's warnings and promises (curses and blessings). Therefore, when we read the prophet's words, what we read is nothing genuinely new, but the same message in essence delivered by God originally through Moses.[6]

Second, Malachi's promise was given to Israel as a nation. It was a corporate, not an individual, promise. Verse 12 states: " 'Then all the nations will call you blessed, for yours will be a delightful land,' says the LORD Almighty." In this context, *you* is clearly Israel, and the *delightful land* is the land of Palestine. God was promising to give economic prosperity to the nation if Israel would be obedient to his covenant.

Third, the promise is related to the Old Testament temple, not the New Testament church. Malachi's reference to *my house* (v. 10) is an allusion to the temple in Jerusalem, not to First Baptist in Peoria. Tithes, in the form of sacrificial animals, grain and fruit, were needed to carry on the temple worship proscribed by law. Modern-day offerings for building programs, missions and pastoral salaries were simply not in view.

Having said all this, might it not be possible to find a general principle in this passage that would be applicable today? After all, finding such principles has been one of the major concerns of this book. Yes, it is possible—even recommended.

For example, one clear principle in the passage is that God rewards obedience. That principle has been affirmed numerous times in both the Old and New Covenants (Ps 19:11; 62:12; Is 40:10; Mt 5:12; 1 Cor 3:14). A second principle is that we should give back a portion of our income to the Lord as an act of worship and obedience. That principle is also reiterated in the New Covenant (1 Cor 16:1-4; 2 Cor 8—9).

We must realize, however, that a principle is not the same as a promise. A principle is usually based on who God *is*—and God never changes; he is the same in both Old and New Covenants. But a promise is based on what God has said he would *do* or not do, and both the conditions and the recipients of his promises have sometimes changed greatly from the Old to the New Covenant.[7]

For example, consider the simple principle "God rewards obedience." Under the New Covenant the type of obedience God requires and the kinds of rewards he offers are very different from those of ancient Israel. Obviously, it would be ludicrous—even impossible—for us to give tithes for the temple in Jerusalem since that temple no longer exists. Therefore, in order to apply the principle in Malachi 3, we need to look into the New Testament to find the conditions and blessings associated with obedience.

But what if a promise is part of the New Covenant? In that case it may or may not apply directly to us, depending on the answers to the other questions we must ask.

To Whom Is the Promise Given?

Someone recently loaned me a little book entitled *God's Promises for Your Every Need*. The book contains biblical promises for such needs as discouragement, worry, loneliness, depression, financial trouble, sickness and marital problems. Although I opened the book with a degree of skepticism, I was genuinely encouraged by many of the promises I read. I can understand why many people would find this kind of book a helpful resource.

Yet I was also discouraged by some of what I saw. All of the promises in the book were isolated from their original contexts, and some of them were clearly taken *out* of context. For example, in the section entitled "Waiting On God," I read the promise: "For the vision is yet for an appointed time, but at the end it shall speak, and not lie: though it tarry, wait for it; because it will surely come, it will not tarry" (Hab 2:3, KJV). Presumably this promise is supposed to assure me that what I am waiting for will come to pass. Yet in its original context it refers to the certainty of the Babylonian invasion of Judah: "I am raising up the Babylonians, that ruthless and impetuous people, who sweep across the whole earth to seize dwelling places not their own" (Hab 1:6)—hardly an encouraging promise!

Before applying a biblical promise, we must identify the person or group to whom the promise was originally given. Unfortunately, this fact is often overlooked by Christians, especially when studying prophetic literature, such as that found in the Habakkuk passage quoted above. Most prophetic books were written directly to Israel and Judah. They warned the people about the impending invasions of Assyria and Babylon and then offered promises of future restoration. We cannot ignore the original audience and historical context of these books without serious danger of misapplying what we read.

If we carefully examine the original audience and context, we discover that there are at least three categories of promises directly intended for us.

Promises that are universal in scope. Some biblical promises apply to everyone in every age—including us. For example, the promises of salvation through Jesus Christ are extended to everyone. John writes: "He is the atoning sacrifice for our sins, and not only for ours but also for the sins of the whole world" (1 Jn 2:2). Likewise, Paul states that "everyone who calls on the name of the Lord will be saved" (Rom 10:13). Even some Old Testament promises have a universal character, such as Isaiah's statement: "Those who hope in the LORD will renew their strength. They will soar on wings like eagles; they will run and not grow weary, they will walk and not be faint" (Is 40:31).

Promises given to the church. Because we are members of the church, we can legitimately conclude that these promises were given for our benefit. For example, in addition to salvation through Jesus Christ, Christians are given the promise of Christ's presence, both now and forever (Mt 28:20); the promise of the Holy Spirit (Acts 2:38); the promise that in all things God works for our good (Rom 8:28); the promise that nothing can separate us from Christ's love (Rom 8:35-39); the promise that God will meet all our needs (Phil 4:19); the promise that we will one day be glorified with Christ (Col 3:4); the promise of his return (Acts 1:11); and the promise that we will live with him forever (Rev 20—21). These and many other promises are part of our inheritance as God's children.

Promises given to other groups to which we belong For example, Paul reminds children of the promise given to them in the Ten Commandments: "Children, obey your parents in the Lord, for this is right. 'Honor your father and mother'—which is the first commandment with a promise—'that it may go well with you and that you may enjoy long life on the earth' " (Eph 6:1-3). This category would also include promises to widows, the fatherless and the poor.[8]

Although many of the promises in the Bible are directly intended for us, many are not. For example, most Old Testament promises were given to Israel. Many other promises in both testaments were given to specific individuals, such as Abraham, Jacob, David or Paul. What do we do with these promises? Do we simply conclude that they were for someone else, or can we legitimately apply them in our own lives? We must evaluate each promise separately to find out.

When seeking to apply promises of this type, we must ask an important question: Is there is any legitimate reason for us to believe that this promise—or others like it—might apply to us today? Can we find any evidence that the promise extends beyond the person or group to whom it was originally given? In the absence of such evidence, we cannot assume a promise applies to us; in fact, we must assume just the opposite. However, in many cases there are good reasons for believing these promises can apply, in a secondary sense, to us today.

For example, many Old Testament promises were based on the covenant God made with Abraham, Isaac and Jacob (see Gen 15). That covenant promised that Abraham's descendants would be as numerous as the stars in the heavens, that they would be given a homeland and that they would be blessed by God. Each of these promises was directly fulfilled during the history of Israel. The Israelites did become numerous during their slavery in Egypt (Ex 1). They were given the land of Palestine as their homeland (Josh 1). And the nation was greatly blessed during various periods (2 Sam 8; 1 Kings 10).

However, the New Testament indicates that these promises did not reach their final fulfillment in Israel. Paul claims that Abraham's descendants are ultimately those who put their faith in Jesus Christ (Rom 4; Gal 3). Likewise, the permanent homeland for Abraham and his descendants is not Palestine but the new heavens and earth (Heb 11:13-16). And the true blessings of Abraham are not temporal and material but spiritual and eternal, the blessings given through Jesus Christ (Gal 3:14, 29).

Of course, some might claim that this kind of application is merely a way of spiritualizing the original promises. I disagree. In many respects Israel represented only an image, a foretaste, of what would be fulfilled ultimately with the coming of Jesus Christ. As we look into the mirror of Israel's history, therefore, it is not surprising that we should see a reflection of greater realities to come.

But what about promises that were given to specific individuals, such as David, Joshua or Paul? Can promises given to them possibly apply to us as well? Once again, that depends on whether there is any specific reason to believe these promises extend beyond those to whom they were originally given. Obviously, the answer to this question will vary from passage to passage.

Consider, for example, the promises God made to Joshua in chapter one of that book. After the death of Moses, Joshua was suddenly given the mantle of leadership. No doubt he was troubled by such thoughts as, "How can I possibly replace Moses? And how can I lead Israel into the most difficult period in its history—the conquest of Canaan?"

In response to these fears and self-doubts, the Lord assures Joshua:

No one will be able to stand up against you all the days of your life. As I was with Moses, so I will be with you; I will never leave you nor forsake you. (v. 5)

Then, to calm any remaining fears, he repeatedly states:

Be strong and courageous, because you will lead these people to inherit the land I swore to their forefathers to give them" (v. 6). "Be strong and very courageous. Be careful to obey all the law my servant Moses gave you" (v. 7). "Have I not commanded you? Be strong and courageous." (v. 9)

The chapter concludes with the same refrain: "Be strong and courageous!" (v. 18).

This chapter has been a great encouragement to me on many occasions, especially when I have felt overwhelmed and fearful about a task I was facing. In such circumstances it is difficult to read the chapter without identifying with Joshua and with the promises God gave him.

But is it really legitimate for me to apply to my situation promises God gave specifically to Joshua? Think for a moment about how the promise is transformed in the process. Suddenly Joshua becomes Jack, the Canaanites become my difficult situation, and conquests on the battlefield become my personal victories. Even the very act of describing this process makes me wonder whether I have simply twisted Scripture for my own purposes.

However, in this case there is good reason to believe the

promise has application today. In the book of Hebrews we discover that the author gives the same assurance to his readers that
the Lord gave to Joshua:

> Keep your lives free from the love of money and be content
> with what you have, because God has said, "Never will I leave
> you; never will I forsake you." So we say with confidence,
> "The Lord is my helper; I will not be afraid. What can man
> do to me?" (Heb 13:5-6)

Notice, however, what is the same and what has changed in this
promise. Obviously, the context of the promise has changed. In
the immediate context, the fear of the battlefield has been replaced by the temptation to love money and to be discontented
with what we have.

Notice too how the promise of physical protection has
changed. Although the statement "The Lord is my helper; I will
not be afraid. What can man do to me?" sounds similar to "No
one will be able to stand up against you all the days of your life,"
in fact the two are quite different. Joshua was promised immediate physical protection and victory in conquering the land of
Palestine. The Hebrews, on the other hand, were promised resurrection (11:35) and a "better country—a heavenly one"
(11:16). Clearly this Old Covenant promise has been reinter-
preted within the context of the New Covenant.[9]

Other aspects of the promise remain the same. God's presence
and protection are guaranteed in both passages. Likewise, in
both passages the Lord wants to calm our fears and give us
confidence. The fact that the promise in Hebrews has been rein-
terpreted does not diminish its power. Just the opposite. The
hope of a resurrection body which, as Paul says elsewhere, will
be immortal and imperishable is far greater than the immediate

protection of our mortal and perishable bodies. Likewise, the promise of a heavenly country—a new heaven and earth—is far greater than the hope of living on a parcel of land in Palestine.

Is the Promise Conditional or Unconditional?

Once we conclude that a promise applies to us, we must also ask whether its fulfillment is dependent in any way on our actions or attitudes. In other words, we must determine whether the promise is conditional or unconditional.

Some of the promises of Scripture are unconditional; that is, they are not ultimately dependent on our obedience or faithfulness. Some have claimed, for example, that God's promises to Abraham were unconditional. The Lord said to Abram:

> I will make you into a great nation and I will bless you; I will make your name great, and you will be a blessing. I will bless those who bless you, and whoever curses you I will curse; and all peoples on earth will be blessed through you. (Gen 12:2-3)

These promises were given to Abram before he had left Ur, before he had believed the Lord and before he had been declared righteous. Although Abram needed to cooperate with God by leaving his homeland and journeying to the Promised Land, his cooperation was not an explicit condition of the promises.

In the same way, certain promises given to us are unconditional. Notice, for example, the powerful language Paul uses to assure us of God's unconditional love:

> I am convinced that neither death nor life, neither angels nor demons, neither the present nor the future, nor any powers, neither height nor depth, nor anything else in all creation, will be able to separate us from the love of God that is in Christ

Jesus our Lord. (Rom 8:38-39)

In the same passage Paul also gives us the unconditional promise of God's help in fulfilling his good purpose for our lives: "What, then, shall we say in response to this? If God is for us, who can be against us? He who did not spare his own Son, but gave him up for us all—how will he not also, along with him, graciously give us all things?" (Rom 8:31-32).

Such promises are extremely encouraging to us, since they are dependent on God's faithfulness rather than our own. Yet many, if not most, of the promises in Scripture have at least some conditions attached to them.

Perhaps one of our greatest dangers as Christians is to overlook or ignore these conditions. We are often so convinced of God's grace and love that we assume it doesn't matter how we act or think—his promises will be fulfilled just the same. As a result, we don't really take God's Word seriously when it makes certain demands of us.

Consider Paul's promise of our being presented spotless before Christ: "He has reconciled you by Christ's physical body through death to present you holy in his sight, without blemish and free from accusation" (Col 1:22).

Some Christians teach that once a person has accepted Christ it doesn't matter how the person lives or what the person believes—he is "eternally secure." However, such people overlook the conditional aspect of Paul's promise—"if you continue in your faith, established and firm, not moved from the hope held out in the gospel" (v. 23).

A very dear friend of mine professed faith in Christ in 1972 after five years of resisting the gospel. Almost overnight he became a completely different person. His wife, who was both moved and frightened, said: "It is as though he has died and someone else is living in his body!"

I telephoned him the day after his conversion. Previously he had hated the apostle Paul, claiming that he was both racist and antifeminist. However, that morning he had read in 2 Timothy 4 about Paul's final imprisonment. He wept for Paul as he read about his suffering, his loneliness, his longing for a cloak to keep him warm and books to occupy his mind. My friend looked across the two-thousand-year gulf that separated him from Paul and embraced him as a brother in Christ.

When I saw my friend a few days later, I discovered his wife had not exaggerated. There was a gentleness about him that had replaced his gruff exterior. There was a humility—especially when he prayed—that had replaced his sometimes-stubborn pride. Although I was joyful at what I saw, I too was somewhat frightened, feeling as though I was privileged to witness a miracle of God.

As the weeks passed, I saw that this was no fleeting mountain-top experience. In obedience to Christ this man who had rarely been in a church gave his testimony to hundreds of people at his baptism. He read and reread the Scriptures from cover to cover. Every day he offered gentle prayers to God and rejoiced at the answers he saw. He witnessed to friends and business associates. He was a better husband and father. I have never known such joy at the work of God in a person's life.

About four years later, however, his faith began to waver. He was offended by the political conservatism of the people in his church. He despised the radio and television evangelists who were always asking for money. He was convinced that science and Scripture conflicted in many areas and felt that science was the more reliable guide.

Yet these were only symptoms of a far deeper struggle. He could not bring himself to believe that his mother, who had died without knowing Christ, was eternally lost. That thought tormented him day and night. So he was faced with a choice—at least at a subconscious level. He could either hold on to Scripture and face the truth about his mother or he could hold on to his mother and reject the teachings of Scripture. Although the decision didn't occur overnight, he chose the latter.

He stopped going to church. A few months later he stopped reading the Bible. Finally, he stopped praying. That was twelve years ago. Today this man who had "tasted the heavenly gift" is an atheist.

The joy I felt at his conversion has only been surpassed by the anguish I feel at his apostasy—for that is what it is. I would like nothing more than to believe that my friend will still be presented "holy in his sight, without blemish and free from accusation" (v. 22). But in order to believe that, I would have to ignore the conditional aspect of Paul's promise. My friend has not continued in the faith; he has rejected it. He has not remained firm in the hope held out in the gospel; he has cast it away. Therefore, I have no assurance that Paul's promise applies to him.

Although I firmly believe in eternal security, I also believe that those who are eternally secure will persevere in the faith. As Paul says, we must not only believe, we must *continue* in the faith.[10]

Is the Promise Qualified by Other Parts of Scripture?

As we seek to apply biblical promises, the final question we must ask is whether the promise is qualified by other parts of Scripture.

In recent years a number of "health and wealth" preachers have gained an enormous following. Their message is a curious blend of the biblical gospel and the American dream. They claim that it is every Christian's spiritual birthright to be both healthy and wealthy.

Although their "theology" is based on a number of passages of Scripture, one passage receives prominent attention. In Mark 11:24 Jesus tells his disciples: "I tell you, whatever you ask for in prayer, believe that you have received it, and it will be yours."

The health-and-wealth teachers view this verse as a blank check given to them by God. They assert that if we truly believe we will receive what we ask for, we can write our own ticket with the Lord. We simply need to "name it and claim it" by faith.[11]

In the area of finances, for example, Christians who claim prosperity by faith can expect to live in mansions and drive Cadillacs. As one preacher brashly put it, "My Father is not in the used-car business."[12]

Yet those who view Mark 11:24 as a spiritual blank check fail to grasp that this promise is qualified, both explicitly and implicitly, by other passages of Scripture. In John 16:23, for example, Jesus explicitly qualifies his earlier promise when he says, "I tell you the truth, my Father will give you whatever you ask in my name." Asking for something "in Jesus' name" means to ask according to his character and will. As John later put it, "This is the confidence we have in approaching God: that if we ask anything according to his will, he hears us" (1 Jn 5:14). Therefore, we cannot assume that God will give us a mansion or a Cadillac simply because we believe hard enough. We must first ask whether they represent his will for our lives.

The promise in Mark is also implicitly qualified by other passages in Scripture. If it is God's will that every Christian be rich, then Jesus and the apostles were not very good examples of their own teaching. In Matthew 8:20 Jesus describes himself in a way that hardly speaks of wealth: "Foxes have holes and birds of the air have nests, but the Son of Man has no place to lay his head." Paul is even more graphic in his description of himself and the other apostles:

> It seems to me that God has put us apostles on display at the end of the procession, like men condemned to die in the arena. We have been made a spectacle to the whole universe, to angels as well as to men. We are fools for Christ, but you are so wise in Christ! We are weak, but you are strong! You are honored, we are dishonored! To this very hour we go hungry and thirsty, we are in rags, we are brutally treated, we are homeless. We work hard with our own hands. When we are cursed, we bless; when we are persecuted, we endure it; when we are slandered, we answer kindly. Up to this moment we have become the scum of the earth, the refuse of the world. (1 Cor 4:9-13)

Did Jesus lack faith in his own promise? If not, then why didn't he own a mansion rather than living without even a place to lay his head? Did the apostles fail to believe God's promise of wealth? If not, then why were they hungry and thirsty, homeless and dressed in rags? Clearly any interpretation of the promise in Mark 11:24 must take these other biblical passages into consideration. We should always interpret Scripture in light of Scripture.

Proverbs and Promises
Before concluding this chapter, I should say a brief word about

proverbs. The book of Proverbs contains many sayings that sound very much like promises. For example, consider the following statements:

Commit to the LORD whatever you do, and your plans will succeed. (Prov 16:3)

Train a child in the way he should go, and when he is old he will not turn from it. (Prov 22:6)

A generous man will prosper; he who refreshes others will himself be refreshed. (Prov 11:25)

Do not love sleep or you will grow poor; stay awake and you will have food to spare. (Prov 20:13)

He who works his land will have abundant food. (Prov 28:19)

In spite of appearances, however, most proverbs—including the ones just quoted—are not promises. They are wise sayings, principles that are generally true of life. Those who follow the advice given in Proverbs will have wisdom for dealing with the practical areas of life.

Unfortunately, many people fail to understand the nature of proverbs. For example, on more than one occasion I have heard Proverbs 22:6 quoted as a promise about child rearing. Some claim this is a guarantee that if we properly raise our children, they will turn out well. Others go so far as to say that if a child becomes rebellious, it is the parents' fault, not the child's. Obviously this view is bound to produce false expectations in some and tremendous guilt in others.

Yet such a position is not difficult to refute. Perhaps the strongest argument against it is the Lord's own experience with his "children," Adam and Eve. Although he was a perfect father to them and provided them with a literal Garden of Eden in which to live, they rebelled against him, bringing the ruin of the human race. Who is to blame for this calamity? Scripture places the responsibility not on God but on man, where it belongs (see Rom 5:12-20).

Or consider the proverb which says: "He who works his land will have abundant food." At the present time, the farmers in our nation are experiencing a serious crisis. Every day we read about those who lose their farms because they cannot pay their bills. To make matters worse, we have just gone through the worst drought since the 1930s. These farmers are working their land as hard as they can, yet many are still facing ruin. If Proverbs 28:19 were a promise, such a situation would be completely inexplicable. However, it is not a promise but a principle, which generally—but not always—holds true.

One additional question might therefore be added to the others considered in this chapter. Before applying a biblical promise, we should ask whether it really *is* a promise.

A Word of Encouragement

I realize that this chapter might better be entitled "How *Not* to Apply Biblical Promises." As I was discussing it with my sister recently, she commented that it all sounded like too much work. She said that most people look for a promise to meet a specific, immediate need in their lives, and that such people would not take the time to think through the questions raised in this chapter.

I agree that a crisis is not the easiest time to be studious and analytical. Yet Scripture taken out of context or misapplied can never be a true help or comfort to anyone. The Bible itself makes it plain that some passages are "hard to understand" and that we can distort the Bible to our own destruction (2 Pet 3:16). Therefore we must be careful and diligent students of the Bible in the quiet times of our lives so that we can be prepared for the crises that inevitably arise. If we do so, we will discover a wealth of promises that *do* apply to our lives, promises which God has given for our comfort, encouragement and hope.

THE LIMITS
OF
APPLICATION

*I*n the previous chapter I mentioned William Miller, that unfor-tunate man who tried to predict that the world would end in 1843. A few years ago I was amazed to hear that history had repeated itself. Two books were written by a man who claimed that the church would be raptured on September 11, 12 and 13 of 1988.[1] (The three separate dates had something to do with the time zones.)

In an article entitled "Doomsayer goofs—but, hey, it's not the end of the world," Dave Barry captured the humor and pain of the event well when he wrote:

I have great news for those of you who were disappointed when the world failed to end last year.

In case you missed it, what happened last year was that a man named Edgar Whisenant, who is a former NASA rocket engineer, came out with a booklet in which he proved via exact mathematical calculations based on the Bible that the world was going to end in 1988, most likely on Sept. 12. . . .

A lot of True Believers around the country got very excited over Mr. Whisenant's prediction, so you can imagine what a letdown it was when Sept. 12 rolled around and—as you know if you keep up with the news—the world did not end. . . .

Well, guess what. Mr. Whisenant has just come out with ANOTHER booklet, and in Chapter 1 (entitled "What Went Wrong in 1988") he graciously admits that there was an error in his calculations. He now scientifically calculates that the world will probably end on—mark it on your appointment calendar—this coming Friday. Yes![2]

There are limits to legitimate application. Yet every day, in countless ways, Christians go beyond these limits. Common sense tells us to avoid some of these excesses, such as closing our eyes and pointing to a verse. But other, more subtle, types of application may escape our notice. These are the ones I wish to focus on in this chapter.

Applications That Go beyond What God Has Revealed

Have you ever wished Scripture were clearer on certain points? Have you ever wanted to ask the apostle Paul what in the world he meant by "baptism for the dead" (1 Cor 15:29), or the author of Hebrews the real meaning of the sixth chapter of the book? I have on many occasions. Unfortunately, we are not always given as much information as we want.

The timing of the Lord's return is obviously one of those

areas. In spite of the fact that Jesus himself said, "No one knows about that day or hour, not even the angels in heaven, nor the Son, but only the Father" (Mt 24:36), people have been trying to predict the day and hour for centuries.

The identity of the antichrist is also a popular area of speculation. At the time of the French Revolution, students of prophetic literature generally agreed that the pope was the antichrist. When I was in seminary, Henry Kissinger was the culprit. People even pointed out that if you added up the numeric value of his name, it equaled 666. Now Soviet General Secretary Gorbachev has been given that dubious distinction. We are confidently told that the birthmark on his forehead is the mark of the beast! Someone recently commented that when Russian leaders treat us badly, they are viewed as dictators of the Evil Empire. And when they treat us well, they are the antichrist. I suppose it is a no-win situation.

It is dangerous to be dogmatic about what Scripture has not revealed. Even a thorough study of the Bible will not give us answers about the timing of the Lord's return or the identity of the antichrist.

We should also be cautious about areas where Scripture is unclear or ambiguous. Unfortunately, Christians have often been most dogmatic about those issues which are least clear. Dispensationalists fight with those of the Reformed tradition over whether there will be an earthly millennium and a "pretribulation rapture." Baptists argue with Presbyterians about whether baptism is for adults or children, and whether it is by immersion or sprinkling. Calvinists debate with Arminians about eternal security and the place of free will.

Although it is certainly proper to have convictions about these matters, we should hold our convictions with humility and an open mind. And we should allow others the freedom of conscience to apply the Scriptures in ways that we feel are wrong or misleading.

Unfortunately, the Bible does not even give us explicit answers to some of the pressing issues of our day. What should our attitude be toward the nuclear arms race? How should we respond to the AIDS epidemic? Should we support or oppose genetic engineering? How can we deal with overpopulation? These and other questions simply were not issues in biblical times. Yet they demand a biblically informed response.

How can we know what to think or do when the Bible gives us no explicit direction? As we look at God's response to issues that *are* covered in Scripture, we will develop spiritual sensitivity to those issues which are not covered. As we listen carefully to what God has said, we will be better equipped when he is silent. Because the Lord has given us his Word and his Spirit, this need not be idle speculation or groping in the dark. In answer to the question "Who has known the mind of the Lord that he may instruct him?" Paul responds with the astounding claim, "But we have the mind of Christ" (1 Cor 2:16).

Applications the Author Never Intended

Imagine, for a moment, that your Sunday-school teacher is giving a series on the evangelistic methods of Paul. In his first lesson he points out that when Paul was in Athens, he went to the synagogue on the Sabbath and the marketplace the other days of the week. He explains that the former was the natural gathering place for Jews, and the latter for Gentiles. He then makes the following application: "Like Paul, we should look for the natural meeting places for non-Christians in our culture. In such places we will often find excellent opportunities for evangelism."

How would you evaluate his application? Is it legitimate or not? Obviously, in one sense it is legitimate. The teacher's comments are insightful and helpful. We would be wise to follow his advice in our evangelism. But does his principle carry the full authority of Scripture? Are we obligated to go to such natural meeting places as a matter of obedience? Does his principle really carry the same weight as, for example, the principle of not causing our brother to stumble?

I think not. The crucial difference is the biblical author's intent. It is doubtful that Luke intended Paul's actions to be normative. He is merely describing what Paul did, not prescribing what we all must do in a similar situation. On the other hand, it is clearly Paul's intent to warn us against causing our brother to stumble. This difference should not be minimized. If an application does not arise out of the divine and human authors' intent, then it does not carry the authority of God's Word, even though it may be helpful and insightful.

Consider another example. Suppose a book is written on the teaching methods of Jesus. The author points out that Jesus was a master storyteller. He used the objects and events of everyday experience to reach his audience. He began with what they knew in order to teach them what they did not know.

Next, the author tells us Jesus frequently used questions in his teaching: "Which is easier: to say to the paralytic, 'Your sins are forgiven,' or to say, 'Get up, take your mat and walk'?" (Mk 2:9). "How can the guests of the bridegroom fast while he is with them?" (v. 19). "Why do you look at the speck of sawdust in your brother's eye and pay no attention to the plank in your own eye?" (Lk 6:41). "Which of these three do you think was a neighbor to the man who fell into the hands of robbers?" (10:36).

The author concludes that in our teaching we should use creative stories that touch on everyday experiences. We should also ask questions of our audience in order to get them to think and to re-examine their beliefs and values.

Is this good advice? Yes! Jesus is the greatest teacher who ever lived, and we would be foolish not to imitate his methods. But is the author's advice the Word of God simply because his examples are drawn from Scripture? No, because it doesn't arise from the Gospel writers' intent. They weren't giving their readers a course in creative Bible teaching; they were presenting Jesus as the Messiah, the Savior of the world. *How* Jesus taught was incidental to their purpose. *What* Jesus said and did was of utmost importance in their minds.

Applications Based on a Faulty Translation or Interpretation

Sometimes our favorite applications are based on a faulty translation or interpretation. For example, one of the most popular passages on guidance is Proverbs 3:5-6: "Trust in the LORD with all your heart and lean not on your own understanding; in all your ways acknowledge him, and he will make your paths straight." The passage seems to be a clear promise of personal guidance, especially when quoted from the King James Version: "and he shall direct thy paths."

Yet concerning this passage, Bruce Waltke writes:

All of us have had the shock of discovering that a favorite verse in the King James Version was inaccurate, and hence that we had been led into an inauthentic experience. I recall the astonishment of one of the committee members assigned to translate the Book of Proverbs for the New International Version when he discovered that Proverbs 3:5 [-6] had nothing to say about guidance. He had taken as his life text: "In all your ways acknowledge Him and He will direct your paths." But when confronted with the linguistic data he had to admit reluctantly that the verse more properly read ". . . and He will make your path smooth."[3]

Certainly, the translation "he will make your paths smooth" does not sound like a promise of guidance. In fact, the New International Version committee did not translate it that way but rather chose "he will make your paths straight," which seems closer to the idea of divine leading. A careful study of the original Hebrew, however, indicates otherwise. Garry Friesen tells us that:

> Hebrew lexicons and commentaries on the Psalms and Proverbs agree that the correct translation of Proverbs 3:6b is: ". . . and He shall make your paths straight, (or) smooth, (or) successful." The noun "path" is frequently employed in the Psalms and Proverbs. But it does not have the idea of an individual will of God. Hebrew writers use it to describe the general course or fortunes of life (see Proverbs 4:18-19; 15:19). When the verb "make straight, make smooth" is connected with the noun "paths," the meaning of the statement is, "He shall make the course of your life successful."[4]

Therefore, even if we are like the man who made this his life text, we must not try to apply Proverbs 3:5-6 to guidance. On both the level of translation and interpretation, it simply will not support that idea.

Another example of an application based on a faulty interpretation is the use of 3 John 2 by those who believe every Christian should be financially wealthy. In the King James Version the verse reads: "Beloved, I wish above all things that thou mayest prosper and be in health, even as thy soul prospereth."

Concerning the popular application of this verse, Bruce Barron writes:

> Ever since Oral Roberts interpreted this passage in this way in the 1950s, charismatic evangelists have quoted the apostle John's words, as translated in the King James Version, as a demonstration of God's desire that we may "prosper and be in health." . . . Yet Christians with stronger backgrounds in biblical study have repeatedly questioned the faith movement's understanding of the verse.
>
> Read in context, 3 John 2 seems to be a personal wish for Gaius, the recipient of John's letter, not a divine promise for all Christians. Pentecostal scholar Gordon Fee has discovered that this verse is "the *standard* form of greeting in a personal letter in antiquity." He concludes, "To extend John's wish for Gaius to refer to financial and material prosperity for all Christians of all times is *totally foreign* to the text."[5]

Whether it is a favorite verse on guidance, a supposed promise of prosperity or whatever, we must be sure our application is based on a proper translation and interpretation of Scripture. Anything else clearly exceeds the proper limits of application.

Applications Based on Faulty Logic

A number of years ago, while I was still in college, I visited the headquarters of a large parachurch organization. That evening about a thousand students gathered to hear a well-known speaker. However, before his talk, he asked all those who knew without a doubt that they were filled with the Holy Spirit to stand up. Nine hundred and ninety-nine students jumped to their feet, while I alone remained seated. I felt like a lion in the Daniel's den!

How could they be so confident that they were filled with the Spirit? Earlier that day they were taught the following spiritual syllogism: (1) God commands us to be filled with the Spirit, so it is his will for us (Eph 5:18); (2) if we ask anything according to God's will, he hears and answers us (1 Jn 5:14-15); (3) therefore, if we ask to be filled with the Spirit we can be absolutely certain we will be.

Sounds flawless, doesn't it? Yet try the same type of logic with these verses: (1) God does not want anyone to perish, but everyone to come to repentance (2 Pet 3:9); (2) if we ask anything according to God's will, he hears and answers us (1 Jn 5:14-15); (3) therefore, if we ask God not to let anyone perish, everyone will be saved. Clearly something is wrong here!

What then was wrong with their logic? Scripture cannot always be forced into neat little syllogisms. The proper way to understand the filling of the Spirit is to make a careful study of the phrase throughout the New Testament.[6]

When we do so, we discover that the only thing common to those who were filled is that they *spoke,* usually in a prophetic fashion, immediately after being filled. They didn't always pray before being filled, nor did their filling always follow an act of surrender to the Lord. In most cases the filling came unexpectedly, as God sovereignly provided what was needed for the occasion (Lk 1:39-45, 67-79; Acts 4:8-12; 7:55-56; 13:9-11).

These findings may not satisfy our desire for formulas and conditions that allow us to control when we are filled with the

Spirit. But they should remind us of our dependence on God, the One who really is in control of the events in our lives.

All That We Need

In 2 Timothy 3:15-16 Paul reminds Timothy that "from infancy you have known the holy Scriptures, which are able to make you wise for salvation through faith in Christ Jesus. All Scripture is God-breathed and is useful for teaching, rebuking, correcting and training in righteousness, so that the man of God may be thoroughly equipped for every good work." Although there are limits to application, the scope of Scripture is immense. For centuries the best scholars in the world have studied the Bible and yet have not begun to plumb its depths. Clearly God's Word does not tell us everything we want to know; but it does tell us everything we need.

THE NEVERENDING STORY

*I*n The Neverending Story *a little boy named Bastian is chased* into a bookstore by bullies. The bookstore owner tells him to go away. "The video arcade is down the street," he says gruffly, "Here we just sell small rectangular objects—they're called *books*. They require a little effort on your part. They make no b-b-b-beeps. On your way, please!"

"I know books," replies Bastian. "I have 186 of them at home."

"Ah, comic books," says the man.

"No! replies Bastian, "I've read *Treasure Island, The Last of the Mohicans, The Wizard of Oz, The Lord of the Rings, Twenty Thousand Leagues Under the Sea, Tarzan. . . .*"

As Bastian moves closer to the man, he notices a strange book lying on the table.

It was bound in copper-colored silk that shimmered when he moved it about. Leafing through the pages, he saw the book was printed in two colors. There seemed to be no pictures, but there were large, beautiful capital letters at the beginning of the chapters. Examining the binding more closely, he discovered . . . an oval. And inside the oval, in strangely intricate letters, he saw the title:

The Neverending Story

"What's that book about?" asks Bastian.

"Oh, this is something *special,*" says the bookstore owner.

"Well, what is it?"

"Look, your books are safe," says the man. "By reading them you get to become Tarzan or Robinson Crusoe."

"But that's what I like about 'em."

"Ah, but afterwards you get to be a little boy again."

"What do you mean?" asks Bastian.

"Listen," says the man, "have you ever been Captain Nemo, trapped inside your submarine while the giant squid is attacking you?"

"Yes."

"Weren't you afraid you couldn't escape?"

"But it's only a story!"

"That's what I'm talking about," says the man, "the ones *you* read are safe."

"And this one isn't?" exclaims Bastian.[1]

Like *The Neverending Story,* the Bible isn't safe. Its words either bring us to life or stand in judgment against us on the Last Day. Like a hot coal, the Bible cannot be picked up without burning its imprint into our lives.

And like *The Neverending Story,* the Bible demands involvement. Later, as Bastian opens the book in the dusty attic of his school, he discovers that he isn't simply reading a story; *he is part of the story.*

What he saw was something quite unexpected, which wasn't the least bit terrifying, but which baffled him . . . He saw a fat little boy with a pale face—a boy his own age—and this little boy was sitting on a pile of mats, reading a book. . . .

Bastian gave a start when he realized what he had just read. Why, that was him! The description was right in every detail. The book trembled in his hands. This was going too far![2]

We cannot read the Bible without becoming part of the story. Our actions and attitudes affect both the plot and the outcome of what God is doing in history.

Have you ever noticed how the book of Acts ends abruptly? For twenty-eight chapters Luke describes the birth and growth of the church as the gospel spreads outward from Jerusalem. Then, quite without warning, he stops. There is no summary, no conclusion. It is as though Luke is telling us the story is incomplete. How *could* it be complete until the gospel is spread throughout the world and the Lord returns? Therefore, Luke invites us to pick up where he and the apostles left off—to become a part of the true Neverending Story.

That is the great joy and challenge of application!

Notes

Introduction

[1]Josh McDowell, *Guide to Understanding Your Bible* (San Bernardino, Calif.: Here's Life Publishers, 1982), p. 100.

[2]For a good summary of recent scholarly discussion about application, see William J. Larkin, Jr., *Culture and Biblical Hermeneutics* (Grand Rapids, Mich.: Baker Book House, 1988), especially pp. 104-113.

[3]John Stott, *Between Two Worlds* (Grand Rapids, Mich.: Eerdmans, 1982), p. 140.

[4]Gordon Fee and Douglas Stuart, *How to Read the Bible for All It's Worth* (Grand Rapids, Mich.: Zondervan, 1982).

[5]Walter A. Henrichsen, *Layman's Guide to Applying the Bible* (Grand Rapids, Mich.: Zondervan, 1985).

Chapter 1: The Goal of Application

[1]*How to Read the Bible,* p. 78.

Chapter 2: Learning to Apply God's Word

[1]I believe that this comedy routine was part of an album called *Beyond the Fringe,* but it has been years since I have heard it.

[2]William Larkin writes: "Where direct application is not warranted by the text, one may look for a principle and a contemporary form compatible with it. Scripture offers examples of such a process. Paul cites a command from Deuteronomy 25:4, 'Do not muzzle an ox while it is treading out the grain,' and goes on to apply the underlying principle to the question of fair pay for Christian workers" *Culture,* p. 316.

I realize that some may still view Paul's use of Deuteronomy as an example of proof-texting, but the practice of finding underlying principles is illustrated elsewhere in Scripture (see, for example, 2 Cor 12:7-10).

[3]*Handbook of Life in Bible Times,* ed. J. A. Thompson (Downers Grove, Ill.: InterVarsity Press, 1986), pp. 130-31.

Chapter 3: Step One: Understanding the Original Situation

[1]*The New Bible Dictionary* (Grand Rapids, Mich: Eerdmans, 1971).

[2]What about the King James Version? It is beautifully written, but I would not recommend it for Bible study. A good translation should cross the language barrier between the biblical world and our own. The KJV did that for those living in the seventeenth century, but for those living today, methinks a four-hundred-year gap doth create unnecessary confusion!

[3]*The Macmillan Bible Atlas* (New York: Macmillan, 1968) is one of the best Bible atlases available.

[4]As quoted by Robert A. Traina, *Methodical Bible Study* (Wilmore, Ky.: Asbury Theological Seminary, 1952), pp. 97-98.

[5]For a fuller discussion of how to study the various types of literature in the Bible, see *How to Read the Bible,* pp. 57-71.

[6]For a good, basic commentary series, I would recommend *The Tyndale New Testament Commentaries* (Grand Rapids, Mich.: Eerdmans) and *The Tyndale Old Testament Commentaries* (Downers Grove, Ill.: InterVarsity Press).

Chapter 4: Step Two: Finding General Principles

[1]The NIV Study Bible (Grand Rapids, Mich.: Zondervan, 1985), note on p. 1519.

[2]It should be strongly emphasized that our love for God and our neighbor does not exhaust the meaning of Scripture. The Bible also speaks a great deal about *God's love for us,* a love which is not in view in the two great commandments. We will consider God's love for us in chapter seven. It should also be noted that Jesus later added a third commandment to the previous two: "My command is this: Love each other as I have loved you" (Jn 15:12). The new objects of this love are our brothers and sisters in Christ. The new standard of love is Christ's sacrificial love for us.

[3]*Handbook,* p. 357.

[4]In the next chapter we will look at how we can tell which practices today would be truly comparable to eating food sacrificed to idols.

[5]*The New Bible Dictionary: Second Edition* (Wheaton, Ill.: Tyndale, 1982), p. 401.

[6]John Stott, *Involvement: Being a Responsible Christian in a Non-Christian Society* (Old Tappan, N. J.: Fleming H. Revell, 1984), p. 59.

[7]*Involvement,* p. 56.

Chapter 5: Step Three: Applying General Principles Today

[1]I realize that in certain passages, such as 1 Corinthians 11:2-16, Christians

disagree about which elements are key and which are variables. I have deliberately avoided discussing such controversial passages because they often generate more heat than light. However, by failing to discuss them, I may give the impression that finding key elements is easier than it sometimes is.
[2]*Expository Thoughts* (Carlisle, PA: Banner of Truth, 1987), p. 313.

Chapter 6: The Importance of Meditation
[1]*An All-Round Ministry* (Carlisle, PA: Banner of Truth, 1960), p. 124.
[2]John Stott, *Between Two Worlds,* p. 220.
[3]E. Glenn Hinson, *Christian Spirituality,* ed. Donald Alexander (Downers Grove, Ill.: InterVarsity Press, 1988), pp. 186-87.
[4]Ibid., p. 187 (emphasis mine).
[5]*Between Two Worlds,* p. 222.

Chapter 7: Applying Biblical Commands
[1]Christopher J. H. Wright, *An Eye for an Eye: The Place of Old Testament Ethics Today* (Downers Grove, Ill.: InterVarsity Press, 1983), pp. 151-59.
[2]See Rom 13:9; 1 Cor 10:14; Eph 6:2; Col 3:9; Tit 2:10; Jas 2:11.
[3]Mt 22:37-40; Mk 12:29-33; Rom 13:8-10; Gal 5:14.
[4]*Understanding and Applying the Bible* (Chicago: Moody Press, 1983), p. 243.
[5]It would be difficult to directly apply this law in our society today. For one thing, it would have to be a recognized part of our agricultural economy, so that the poor and aliens would know that such resources were available to them. Yet even if they were available, most poor people would not know how to prepare the grain for consumption. Even so, the principle behind the law has had encouraging results in cities where nonprofit agencies collect surplus food from restaurants and supermarkets and make it available to the poor.
[6]It is possible, of course, for someone today to be in the identical situation faced by the young ruler. After all, many rich people have made wealth their god. Are such people required, therefore, to sell all that they have and give to the poor? That depends. If they can truly put Christ first in their lives without selling their wealth, then selling all that they have would be unnecessary. The New Testament indicates that at least some rich people retained their wealth (see, for example, 1 Timothy 6:17-19).

Chapter 8: Applying Biblical Examples
[1]The NIV Study Bible, ed. Kenneth Barker (Grand Rapids, Mich.: Zondervan, 1985), p. 1363.

Chapter 9: Applying Biblical Promises

[1]As quoted by Anthony A. Hoekema, *The Four Major Cults* (Grand Rapids, Mich.: Eerdmans, 1963), p. 89.

[2]Ibid., p. 91.

[3]Bruce Barron, *The Health and Wealth Gospel* (Downers Grove, Ill.: InterVarsity Press, 1987), p. 21.

[4]George Mallone, *Furnace of Renewal* (Downers Grove, Ill.: InterVarsity Press, 1981), p. 145.

[5]*How to Read the Bible,* p. 151.

[6]Ibid., p. 154.

[7]Of course, God's promises are also a reflection of his character. But the changing nature of his requirements and rewards makes the application of Old Testament promises difficult.

[8]Widows: Deut 10:18; Ps 146:9; the fatherless: Ps 10:14; 68:5; the poor: Ps 14:6; 35:10; Is 14:30; 25:4; 61:1.

[9]It is clear from Hebrews 11 that many Old Testament saints also looked beyond the shadows of Old Covenant promises to the greater realities promised in the New Covenant.

[10]It would be completely wrong to suppose that our perseverance somehow merits our salvation or preserves our eternal security. On the contrary, our perseverance is merely the outward evidence of a genuine inward work of God in our lives. From beginning to end, salvation is by faith, not by endurance. I should also add that as long as my friend is alive, there is still hope that he will return to Christ. That is my prayer!

[11]*Health and Wealth,* p. 71.

[12]Hobart Freeman as quoted in *Health and Wealth,* p. 22.

Chapter 10: The Limits of Application

[1]Edgar C. Whisenant, *88 Reasons Why The Rapture Will Be In 1988* and *On Borrowed Time* (Nashville, TN: World Bible Society, 1988).

[2]Dave Barry, "Doomsayer goofs—but, hey, it's not the end of the world," *Sunday: The Chicago Tribune Magazine,* August 27, 1989, p. 37.

[3]As quoted by Garry Friesen, *Decision Making & the Will of God* (Portland, Ore.: Multnomah Press, 1980), p. 99.

[4]Ibid., p. 98.

[5]*Health and Wealth,* p. 92.

[6]Of course, a thorough study of the filling of the Spirit would also require that we look at the Old Testament. However, such a study goes beyond my purposes in this chapter.

Epilog: The Neverending Story

[1]Michael Ende, *The Neverending Story* (New York: Doubleday & Company, 1983), p. 6. Only the blocked quote is from the book; the dialog is from the movie version of the same name.

[2]Ibid., pp. 90-91.